D1271717

★ ★ ★ IN THE CABINET ★ ★ ★

Secretaries of State: Making Foreign Policy

In 1975, Secretary of State Henry Kissinger (left) conferred with Anwar Sadat (1918-1981), president of Egypt from 1970 to 1981. Meeting with the leaders of other countries is one of many important tasks that U.S. presidents may assign to their secretaries of state.

★★★ IN THE CABINET ★★★

Secretaries of State: Making Foreign Policy

Jason Richie

The Oliver Press, Inc.
Minneapolis

The Oliver Press, Inc.
Charlotte Square
5707 West 36th Street
Minneapolis, MN 55416-2510

Library of Congress Cataloging-in-Publication Data
Richie, Jason, 1966-
Secretaries of State : making foreign policy / Jason Richie.
p. cm. — (In the cabinet ; 1)
Includes bibliographical references (p.) and index.
  Summary: Examines the lives and accomplishments of eight sec-
retaries of state: John Quincy Adams, William Seward, John Hay,
Charles Evans Hughes, Dean Acheson, John Foster Dulles, Henry
Kissinger, and James Baker.
ISBN 1-881508-65-X (lib. bdg.)
1. Statesmen—United   States—Biography—Juvenile
literature. 2. Cabinet officers—United States—Biography—
Juvenile literature. 3. United States—Foreign relations—Juvenile
literature. 4. United States. Dept. of State—Officials and employ-
ees—Biography—Juvenile literature. [1. Cabinet officers. 2.
Statesmen. 3. United States—Foreign relations.] I. Title.
E183.7 .R43 2000
327.73'092'2—dc21
                           99-086502
                              CIP
                              AC

ISBN 1-881508-65-X
Printed in the United States of America

08 07 06 05 04 03 02   8 7 6 5 4 3 2 1

CONTENTS

★ ★ ★ ★

INTRODUCTION

From Isolationism to Internationalism

"We must all hang together," Benjamin Franklin warned as he stooped to sign the Declaration of Independence in 1776, "or assuredly we shall all hang separately." With that, the United States, with little more in its arsenal than a burning desire for freedom from the "Old World" of Europe, declared its independence from Great Britain. Failure to "hang together" and wrestle free, as Franklin noted, would have meant a sudden end to the colonial leaders and their republican experiment. At the time, the most common punishment for treason, or disloyalty to the mother country, was hanging.

Long after the United States won its independence in 1782, its leaders continued to preach complete freedom from the affairs of Europe. John Adams had set the tone in 1776 when he insisted "we should make no treaties of alliance with any European power," but rather "separate ourselves, as far as possible and as long as possible, from all European politics and wars." Adams, who served as president from 1797 to 1801, was the most knowledgeable in foreign affairs among the founders and is usually given credit for formulating the doctrine of isolation followed by the United States until after World War II.

In 1796, President George Washington gave his hallowed stamp of approval to isolationism in his farewell address. "Why . . . " he asked, "entangle our peace and

isolationism: a foreign policy that avoids interfering in the affairs of other countries unless the interests of one's own nation are directly threatened

internationalism: a foreign policy that seeks involvement with other countries through economic cooperation and political influence

republican: of or relating to a nation that has a political system in which a body of citizens elects representatives who are responsible to them

Benjamin Franklin (in front of table, far right) stands with fellow delegates to the Continental Congress as they prepare to sign the Declaration of Independence.

Thomas Jefferson (1743-1826), the first secretary of state, thought the U.S. should avoid getting involved in wars in Europe. Later, Jefferson was elected the third U.S. president.

George Washington (1732-1799), the first president of the United States, did not think that the U.S. should have special attachments to any other country.

prosperity in the toils of European ambition, rivalship, interest . . . or caprice?" The new nation's "true policy," he concluded, should be "to steer clear of permanent alliances with any portion of the foreign world." Thomas Jefferson, upon assuming the office of president in 1801, concurred: "peace, commerce, and honest friendship with all nations, entangling alliances with none."

Clearly, isolation was the ideal that early American leaders sought. But what made them think that they could avoid the conflicts of the Old World indefinitely? European countries had been fighting with one another constantly throughout history, but, as Jefferson noted in his inaugural speech, the United States was "kindly separated by nature and a wide ocean from the exterminating havoc of one quarter of the globe." Washington had seen it, too. "Our detached and distant situation," he had pointed out, "invites and enables us to pursue a different course [than the Europeans]." Its favorable location, then, separated the new nation from the continuous quarrels of European monarchs and leaders.

To keep Europeans from interfering with the New World, the United States had the world's strongest navy protecting its shores. And it cost the Americans nothing. That's because the navy was Great Britain's. The British had two reasons for protecting the Western Hemisphere from the other European powers. First, they still retained interests there (such as Canada). Also, any territorial gain by a European rival (especially France) in the New World would probably make that power even stronger in the Old. The end result was a Royal Navy shield protecting the United States.

As late as the Civil War (1861-1865), the U.S. Navy was less than one-tenth the size of the Royal Navy. The U.S. Army at the time was equally unimposing, with the overwhelming majority of its 16,000 soldiers guarding white westerners against Indian uprisings. (European nations, with no ocean buffers for protection, maintained armies numbering in the hundreds of thousands.) The cost to Americans of maintaining their freedom against foreign invasion was so low between the War of 1812 and World War II (1941-1945) that one historian has described the era as one of "free security."

After World War II, however, isolation from the tangled web of European politics was no longer possible. New weapons like battleships, long-range bomber aircraft, and ballistic missiles had rendered U.S. ocean barriers less formidable. And British power, long a force for global stability, was declining rapidly. When in 1947 British leaders informed their American counterparts that they could no longer afford to protect the government of Greece from communist encroachment, the Americans accepted responsibility for what they believed was a global battle for freedom. In extending a hand to Greece, the U.S. stated its commitment to defending freedom not only in the Western Hemisphere, but also throughout the world.

battleship: one of the largest warships, with the most guns and heaviest armor

ballistic missile: a rocket that is allowed to fall freely, following a path like a thrown ball, after being launched and reaching a predetermined location under rocket power

The cabinet was not specifically established by the U.S. Constitution, although "executive departments" are mentioned as being under the president's jurisdiction in Article II. The cabinet came into being quickly, however, during the first session of Congress in 1789. It consisted of four departments: state, war, treasury, and justice. (The term "cabinet" was not used until the next decade.) Over the years, the cabinet evolved and expanded through custom and is now defined by statute law. The president nominates cabinet secretaries and may remove them from office. The Senate must approve the president's nominations.

diplomat: a person appointed to represent his or her government in relations with the governments of other nations

Secretaries of State: Making Foreign Policy follows the lives and careers of eight of America's most important secretaries of state. As head of the Department of State, the secretary not only acts as liaison between the president and other heads of state, but he or she also typically acts as the president's primary foreign policy advisor. While most presidents have firmly controlled their secretaries through the years, many strong-willed cabinet officials have managed to shape policy to as great an extent as their bosses. Nowhere has this been more true than in the State Department.

The history of U.S. foreign policy can be divided into two parts. During the first period, from 1789 to 1947, the principle of "isolation" guided diplomats. One of the most prominent secretaries of state during this time was John Quincy Adams, who served from 1817 to 1825. Son of the second president and later to become the sixth president, Adams gathered various isolationist sentiments from past leaders like Washington and Jefferson and formed them into an easy-to-follow road map—the Monroe Doctrine—for himself and future leaders. Other notable secretaries of the period include William Henry Seward, head of the State Department from 1861 to 1869; John Milton Hay, secretary of state during the period 1898-1905; and Charles Evans Hughes, chief diplomat from 1921 to 1925.

Since 1947, the United States has embraced "internationalism," the belief that the country should participate in affairs involving more than just the Western Hemisphere. Secretary of State Dean Gooderham Acheson, who wrote the Truman Doctrine in 1947, is this period's most notable American diplomat. Whereas the Monroe Doctrine limited U.S. concern to the Western Hemisphere, the Truman Doctrine argued that American interests had expanded to include the entire world. Subsequent secretaries of state such as John Foster Dulles, Henry Alfred Kissinger, and

James Addison Baker III all dealt with the consequences of Acheson's internationalist policies.

Finally, the epilogue of *Secretaries of State: Making Foreign Policy* examines the international landscape since the fall of the Soviet Union in 1991 and the terrorist attacks of September 11, 2001, on New York City and the Pentagon. While no one can predict the future, one thing seems certain—the era of U.S. free security and isolation is over. The continued existence and proliferation of nuclear weapons and an increasingly integrated global economy mean the United States will never again be able to shield itself from foreign entanglements.

After developing the atomic bomb during World War II, the United States used the weapon to destroy the Japanese city of Hiroshima, pictured here after the 1945 blast. By the early twenty-first century, at least seven other nations also had the ability to wage nuclear war.

JOHN QUINCY ADAMS

The Monroe Doctrine and Isolationism

The Russian tsar, Alexander I, often strolled alone through the streets of St. Petersburg. He occasionally bumped into American diplomat John Quincy Adams. One frosty March day in 1812 when the two men met, Alexander lamented (as Adams later recorded in his journal), "And so it is that, after all, war is coming which I have done so much to avoid. . . . Everything points toward war. *He* keeps on advancing. He began by taking Swedish Pomerania—now has just occupied Prussia—he can't advance much farther without attacking us."

The "he" that the Russian tsar referred to was Napoleon Bonaparte, the self-declared leader of France. Thanks to Napoleon's manipulations, the United States was also on the verge of war—but with Great Britain. As far as Adams was concerned, European politics was an "inextricable labyrinth"—a twisted and corrupt maze that he warned his country "not to involve ourselves in." His years in Russia and diplomatic postings in several other European countries would later influence his tenure as secretary of state.

The Formative Years

The child was born on July 11, 1767, the very day his great-grandfather, John Quincy, died. To honor the deceased, John Adams, future president of the United

John Quincy Adams (1767-1848) wrote the Monroe Doctrine, which outlined the policy of avoiding involvement in European affairs that would guide U.S. presidents and secretaries of state for many years to come.

The Battle of Bunker Hill actually took place on nearby Breed's Hill, which was occupied by American forces. The attacking British army suffered severe losses before the American soldiers ran out of ammunition and were forced to give up the hill. Despite this loss, the damage done to the British gave the Americans confidence to continue their resistance.

States, and Abigail Adams, his wife, named their son John Quincy Adams.

Not quite eight years old in June 1775, John climbed a hill on the family farm in Braintree, near Boston, Massachusetts, and watched American patriots fight British "redcoats" at Bunker Hill. He never forgot seeing the light of cannon fire as men fought and died for freedom.

Early on, John and Abigail believed their son was destined for high public office, perhaps as a great diplomat. In 1778, when the Continental Congress assigned John Adams to be a diplomat to Paris, France, he seized the opportunity to expose his son to the inner workings of international relations.

Thus began a seven-year journey through the capitals of Europe for John Quincy Adams. He followed his father from one posting to another, soaking up what he could of different languages, customs, and literature. The boy grew comfortable with his father's friends—colonial minister to France Benjamin Franklin; future secretary of state and president Thomas Jefferson; and future chief justice of the U.S. Supreme Court John Jay. Young Adams met foreign leaders and studied their nations' diplomatic rules. He learned to despise the absolute power with which the monarchs of Europe ruled, forever dragging their peoples into wars based on their own whims. Better if the United States just avoided the affairs of the continent altogether.

In the spring of 1785, Adams returned to Boston to prepare himself to enter Harvard College. He studied hard and was admitted in March 1786. He graduated a year later, self-assured and ready to make his mark. The bloody French Revolution, which started in 1789, offered him the opportunity. As thousands of wealthy people perished under the guillotine in Paris—including King Louis XVI and his wife, Marie Antoinette—the monarchs of Europe grew fearful that the uprising would sweep them away. They allied in war against France in 1793. When President George Washington proclaimed U.S. neutrality in the conflict, Adams declared his support for Washington's policy. As "a nation at a vast distance from the continent of Europe," he wrote in a Boston newspaper, "it is our duty to remain, the peaceable and silent, though sorrowful spectators of the sanguinary [bloody] scene." The letter proved popular with the public; soon Adams was endorsing other aspects of Washington's foreign policy. The president took note—after all, the young man was the son of his vice president—and nominated Adams to the post of minister to the Netherlands in May 1794.

During his year in the Netherlands, Adams was among the first Americans to warn that French leaders might attempt to maneuver the United States into war against

During his diplomatic career, John Adams (1735-1826) helped to draw up the Treaty of Paris, which ended the American Revolution.

minister: a diplomat ranking just below an ambassador

The French Revolution

Tired of living under a feudal economic system ruled by the French nobility and clergy, the common people joined a growing middle class in 1789 to create a National Assembly. They vowed not to disband without writing a new constitution. French king Louis XVI was forced by public unrest to recognize the Assembly.

Meanwhile, a shortage of food and fear of an aristocratic conspiracy against them had led to rising tensions among the commoners. In reaction to the *grande peur* (great fear), on July 14 a mob in Paris occupied and destroyed the Bastille, a prison that symbolized the power of the king. Violence swept through France as wealthy homes were pillaged and burned. Later, thousands were executed, including the king.

The French revolutionaries made several attempts at establishing a republic before falling to the rule of one man: a general named Napoleon Bonaparte. He called himself first consul until declaring himself emperor in 1804.

Many European countries opposed the overthrow of the monarchy in France, leading to the French Revolutionary Wars (1792-1802). Later, Napoleon's desire for conquest caused what became known as the Napoleonic Wars (1803-1815). The War of 1812 between the U.S. and Britain arose in part out of these European conflicts.

While attempting to flee from France in 1791, King Louis XVI and Queen Marie Antoinette were arrested at Varennes. They, like many aristocrats, were tried for treason and beheaded by the new French government.

John Quincy Adams in 1796, the year before his father became president of the United States

Great Britain, France's archrival. Washington valued his young minister's commonsense advice, even telling the elder Adams that his son "must not think of retiring from the walk of life he is in." Later, Washington would tell John Adams that his son would "prove himself to be the ablest of all our diplomatic corps."

Several diplomatic postings followed, including some under his father, who became the second president of the United States in 1797. Then, John Adams lost the 1800 election to Thomas Jefferson, and John Quincy's successful career suddenly seemed to end. The new administration, the first composed of Republicans after eight straight of the Federalists, might have offered a job to the son of the outgoing Federalist president, but his father ordered him home. Both father and son left public service.

John Quincy Adams soon tired of private life. He won election to the Massachusetts state senate in April 1802,

Although James Madison (1751-1836), the fourth president of the United States, held Federalist ideas, he supported Thomas Jefferson, a Republican leader, and served under him as secretary of state.

The two major political parties during John Quincy Adams's career were the Federalists and the Republicans (also called Jeffersonian Republicans). The Federalists, whom Adams started out supporting, advocated a strong central government. Later, Adams joined the Republicans, who preferred a limited federal government and praised the virtues and abilities of the common people. The Federalists disbanded in 1824; the Jeffersonian Republicans evolved into the present-day Democratic Party.

and, 10 months later, to the U.S. Senate. At 35, Adams was only five years older than the minimum age for serving. He remained a senator until May 1808, when incessant attacks from the Federalist Party on some of his positions forced Adams's resignation. By that time, Adams no longer felt like a member of any party. He wanted to represent the entire nation. The new president, James Madison, took advantage of Adams's split with the Federalists and appointed him minister to Russia in March 1809.

As Adams spent the next six years in St. Petersburg, French emperor Napoleon Bonaparte continued to dominate Europe. To disrupt French trade, Great Britain had been using its powerful navy to blockade the continent since 1806. Napoleon retaliated by capturing neutral ships that honored the British blockade. Caught in the crossfire were the trade-dependent Americans, who blamed Great Britain for disrupting their commerce. The shrewd Napoleon played on this anger, hoping to instigate a conflict between the British and their former colonies. He stopped seizing neutral vessels in late 1810. When the British refused to ease their blockade to allow U.S. trade with Europe, Congress declared war in June 1812.

Adams did not want war. He was sure Napoleon had kindled the conflagration to weaken the British. It was just the type of political maneuvering Adams detested. Besides, he was sure the long struggle with France was bankrupting Britain. In just a few years, Britain's New World possessions (especially in North America) would fall to the United States by default, Adams believed. As it was, the U.S. bumbled along in the war, barely escaping defeat. Fortunately for the United States, the British were

During the War of 1812, the British burned government buildings in Washington, D.C., in retaliation for similar acts by the Americans in Canada.

too preoccupied fighting Napoleon in Europe to capitalize on U.S. mistakes. As Britain neared victory over the French in April 1814, the British grew anxious to turn their full attention to rebuilding Europe; they agreed to peace talks with the United States in Ghent, Belgium. President James Madison chose Adams to lead the American delegation.

The treaty Adams signed resolved none of the war's major causes. However, it gave no territory to the British. Americans rejoiced; once again they had survived a fight with the world's greatest empire. Surely theirs was a chosen country on a path to greatness. Furthermore, they now recognized John Quincy Adams, the hero of Ghent, as their ablest diplomat.

Napoleon Bonaparte leads his men out of Russia after being defeated in 1813.

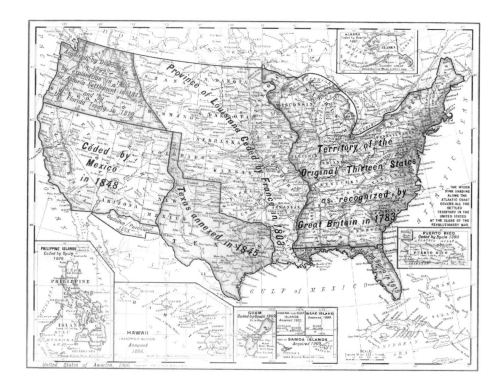

In the Cabinet

In April 1817, Adams received a letter from President James Monroe offering him the post of secretary of state. Adams's first priority after assuming office in September was to help the United States grow stronger. For that to happen, he believed the nation had to grow—period. The Louisiana Purchase of 1803 had more than doubled the size of the United States—a great start, but the Europeans still maintained threatening footholds on the continent. To the north lay British Canada; to the south, southeast (in Florida), and west, Spanish territories including Mexico. Far beyond the Louisiana territory's northwestern fringe, the encroaching hand of Russia reached out to the rich fur reserves in the Pacific Northwest. It was Adams's goal to maneuver the Europeans off the continent.

He targeted Spain first. The Spanish claimed all land west of the Mississippi River, an assertion Adams and

This map shows the location of the Louisiana Purchase, in roughly the center of the current United States. When the French signed the treaty selling their territory to the United States in 1803, no clear boundaries had been outlined. Still, the purchase was certain to include the western half of the Mississippi River Valley and the precious mouth of the Mississippi itself.

James Monroe (1758-1831), the fifth president of the United States, chose John Quincy Adams as his secretary of state.

Monroe flat-out ignored because it would have negated the Louisiana Purchase. Instead, in January 1818, Adams offered Spain all land roughly west of 104 degrees longitude, a generous proposal that represented about one-third of today's United States. Adams did not fear that Spain's acceptance of the offer would end his dream of peacefully conquering the whole of North America. Spain was an empire in decline. Adams believed it to be only a matter of time before any land the Spanish acquired slipped back into American hands.

While Spain considered its options, Secretary of State Adams initiated talks with Great Britain regarding British Canada's boundary with the United States. In October 1818, the two countries drew the border westward along the 49-degree latitude line from present-day northern Minnesota to the Rocky Mountains. All territory east of the Rockies and south of 49 degrees went to the United States (with Spanish territory beginning farther south).

Ownership of the land west of the Rockies—Oregon territory—was left undecided. Here, again, Adams expected that one day Oregon would fall peacefully to the United States.

Adams returned to the problem of the Spanish. They had rejected his and Monroe's earlier proposal. Adams now offered less—a boundary running northwest from the Gulf of Mexico, through the heart of Texas, to a point near the north-central border of present-day Colorado. From there, the line ran due west along the 42nd parallel to the Pacific Ocean. The Spanish knew this was Adams's best and last offer. They had drained their treasury to resist Napoleon's invasion of the Iberian peninsula, which Spain shared with Portugal. Now they faced colonial uprisings in Central and South America. To make matters worse, 3,000 soldiers under General Andrew Jackson had just invaded Florida to halt Indian raids originating from that territory.

After entering Florida, Andrew Jackson and his troops occupied the city of Pensacola, which was the stronghold of Spanish rule.

The Spanish claimed Florida, but Jackson's success there revealed just how weak they were in North America. Spain signed the Transcontinental Treaty in February 1819, ceding Florida and accepting Adams's boundary to the Pacific.

Now that it stretched to the West Coast, the Union was stronger than ever before—yet threats still existed. In the far northwest, Tsar Alexander I claimed present-day Alaska (known as Russian America at the time) and a hefty chunk of western Canada all the way down to 51 degrees latitude. In 1821, the tsar warned all foreign shipping not to sail within 100 miles of the coast of Russian America. Soon afterward, the Russian minister to the United States "suggested" that Americans not trade north of the 51st parallel. This was more than Adams could stand. Freedom of the seas and of trade were vital to America's survival and ability to prosper. The secretary issued a stern protest. The tsar, ever mindful that friendship with the U.S. gave him leverage against the other European powers, quietly dropped the 100-mile prohibition. The ominous Russian presence, however, remained.

Due south of Russian America, the British refused to vacate Oregon. Offshore, fishing and whaling provided growing profits, while thick forests overlooking the ocean offered fur trappers a lucrative hunting ground. Snaking several hundred miles inland from the Oregon coast was the mighty Columbia River, a highway of commerce linking the interior to the sea. From there, trade continued westward to the increasingly profitable Asian market.

Still farther south, Spain was losing control in the Latin American colonies of Mexico, Colombia, Argentina, Chile, and Peru. Leaders in Washington rejoiced—until a rumor circulated that Europe's "Holy Alliance" of Russia, Austria, and Prussia intended action with France to reinstate Spain's rule in the Western Hemisphere. (Tsar Alexander of Russia had initiated the alliance in 1815 to snuff out republican uprisings of the type that had launched the French Revolution and Napoleon's rule.) Before the uprisings,

Alexander I (1777-1825), the Russian tsar from 1801 to 1825

Adams had been concerned only with North America. By 1823, however, he had come to realize that a return of European rule anywhere in the Western Hemisphere would threaten the well-being of the United States.

The administration's response to these concerns in Russian America, in Oregon, and in Latin America was the Monroe Doctrine, written mostly by Adams and proclaimed by the president before Congress on December 2, 1823. Monroe first warned that North and South America "are henceforth not to be considered as subjects for future colonization by any European power." He next reiterated the traditional U.S. policy of avoiding Europe's affairs: "In the wars of the European powers, in matters relating to

Latin America includes those parts of the Western Hemisphere south of the United States that were settled by Spaniards and Portuguese and are now populated mainly by their descendants.

President James Monroe (standing) discusses the Monroe Doctrine with his cabinet, including his secretary of state, John Quincy Adams (far left). Also pictured are (left to right) Secretary of the Treasury William H. Crawford; Attorney General William Wirt; John Caldwell Calhoun and Samuel Southard, secretaries of war and navy, respectively; and Postmaster General John McLean.

themselves, we have never taken any part, nor does it comport with our policy, so to do." Finally, in reference to the Holy Alliance, Monroe declared, "we should consider any attempt on [Europe's] part to extend their system to any portions of this hemisphere, as dangerous to our peace and safety." The message seemed clear enough: the United States would remain withdrawn in "its" hemisphere and avoid interacting with Europe.

Looking Forward

Adams's career as chief diplomat ended in March 1825, when he succeeded Monroe as president. Adams's single term in the White House was not successful. Besides being antislavery, Adams favored internal improvements (like the construction of canals and roads) and a high tariff on imports—all positions that Southern legislators either detested or cared little about. Not much of what the embattled president proposed was actually passed. Adams lost the 1828 presidential election to Andrew Jackson, but did not long remain out of public service. He entered the House of Representatives in 1831, where he served until his death in 1848.

The Monroe Doctrine was never ratified by Congress or made part of international law. The term "Monroe Doctrine" was not even generally used until the 1850s, after the death of both Monroe and Adams. Yet the doctrine lived on, and its principles influenced U.S. foreign policy for almost another century. As the U.S. hunger for land and influence grew in the last half of the nineteenth century, the doctrine became associated not only with excluding European interference in the Americas, but also with the expansion of U.S. power in the hemisphere. Several presidents used this extended interpretation of the Monroe Doctrine to intervene in affairs in Latin American countries. Franklin Delano Roosevelt, president from 1932 to 1945, redefined the doctrine as multilateral—an understanding to be applied by all countries in the Western Hemisphere acting together.

international law: a loose set of guidelines that are generally accepted among nations as applying to their relations with each other

John Quincy Adams suffered a stroke while on the floor of the House and died on February 23, 1848.

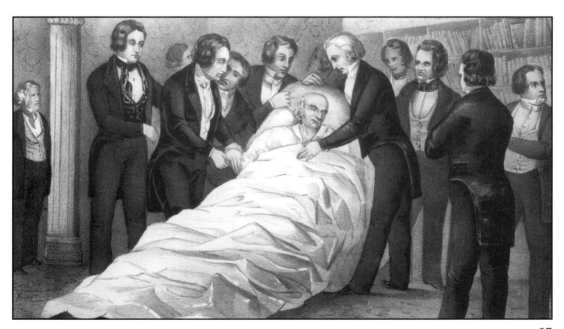

★ ★ *2* ★ ★

WILLIAM HENRY SEWARD

The Civil War and Peaceful Expansion

The death of John Quincy Adams in 1848 shook William Henry Seward. As he told one gathering, Adams had been "a patron, a guide, a counselor, and a friend—one whom I loved scarcely less than the dearest relations." Seward had supported Adams in the presidential race of 1824. Both had favored new programs in education, the construction of canals and highways, and a strong Union. Both hated slavery. And both believed that the U.S. political system, despite the blemish of slavery, was the best in the world.

It's no surprise, then, that Seward sought to continue Adams's lifework—extending U.S. power. Given "fifty, forty, thirty more years of life," Seward proclaimed in 1867, he could secure for the United States all of North America and "control of the world." Like his mentor, Seward hoped to achieve expansion without force of arms. If the Union took up "the cross of republicanism" faithfully and bore it before the world, he was sure surrounding nations would willingly seek annexation. Those not so inclined would certainly adopt the U.S. political system. The future United States, as the "most important and benefi- cent among the powers of the earth," would then go forth to advance global progress.

William Henry Seward (1801-1872) helped main- tain the Union by keeping foreign countries out of the Civil War. He also signifi- cantly improved U.S. relations with Great Britain.

The Formative Years

William Henry Seward was born on May 16, 1801, in the hamlet of Florida, New York. The fourth of six children, "Harry" (as he preferred to be called) was the least healthy of the bunch. His weak condition became an asset, though. Samuel and Mary Seward decided that if they could afford to send just one of their four sons to college, it would be Harry, the least likely to earn a living through manual labor. In 1820, the 19-year-old graduated with highest honors from Union College, a small school near Albany, the capital of New York.

Harry "read law" (worked as an apprentice lawyer) in an Albany law office for the next two years. Near the end of 1822, he accepted a position at a law firm in Auburn, New York. After courting several women, Harry married Frances Adeline Miller, daughter of the firm's senior lawyer, on October 20, 1824.

Soon after the wedding, "Henry" Seward—Frances hated the name "Harry"—cast his vote for John Quincy Adams for president. It was a time of great national confidence. The United States was young, prosperous, and itching to expand its influence—much the same as Seward, who, over the next few years, grew restless in his cramped law office. As far back as the War of 1812, he had followed the actions of the federal government with great interest. In 1828, he dived into the fray. Although he failed in his bid for a seat in the U.S. House of Representatives, he won a seat in the New York state senate two years later. Not yet 30, Seward was its youngest member.

From the beginning, the rough-and-tumble world of politics consumed Seward. When his senate term expired in 1834, the up-and-comer ran for governor as a member of the new Whig Party. Unfortunately for him, the Democrats, with ex-general Andrew Jackson in the White House, were at the zenith of their popularity. They swept most races that year, including New York's gubernatorial

During the winter of 1833-1834, the newly formed Whig Party was a loose coalition of various movements brought together by a common distrust of influential politicians, especially Andrew Jackson. Because the Whigs never formed a solid party platform, they quickly broke into factions when slavery became an important issue in the United States. The antislavery Whigs were termed "Conscience" Whigs, while those who were proslavery were named "Cotton" Whigs.

contest. Seward slipped back into his unfulfilling law practice, but he remained fixated on the governorship. As the leader of a powerful state, Seward could expect a national following. It was his ultimate goal to ride that fame someday right into the White House.

Seward based his second run for governor on improving education and transportation. Better education, he argued, would end crime and racial and political intolerance. A tighter transportation network of roads, rails, and waterways would bind the nation together, helping to end regional differences that periodically threatened to split the Union. The hopeful message struck the right chord and Seward was victorious in 1838.

Over the next four years, he improved New York's canal and rail systems and reformed the public schools.

Meant to contrast Seward's leniency with the Democrat-controlled New York prison administration's harsh practices, this political cartoon shows a prisoner pleading to see a priest. The priest shows a letter of permission to enter from Seward, but the guard refuses to let him in.

His popularity gained him election to the U.S. Senate in 1848. By the late 1850s, Seward sat on the Senate Foreign Relations Committee, where he wielded much influence as a member of the upstart Republican Party. Barring the emergence of some unexpected rival, Seward seemed ready to capture the presidency in 1861.

He had positioned himself well, with a favorable national reputation and the respect of powerful Senate colleagues. He was adamantly antislavery and made many speeches explaining his position. Although this made him unpopular with Southerners, he had substantial support in the North. In the end, however, Republicans branded Seward less "electable" than another—Abraham Lincoln from Illinois. New York, Seward's state, was considered safely Republican, so Lincoln, from a toss-up state the Republicans needed to win for victory in the general election, captured the nomination.

The Republican delegates to the 1860 convention in Chicago thought that Abraham Lincoln (1809-1865) represented the "common man" better than Henry Seward did.

Switching Parties

During Seward's rise as a politician, politics within parties was often based on personal likes and dislikes of others rather than on issues. Most people shifted allegiance often, Seward included. As a boy, he was a Federalist, but, disappointed with the party's attitude toward the War of 1812, he became a National Republican in 1824. The National Republicans supported John Quincy Adams for president. By 1828, Seward had joined the Antimasons, which he called "the party of the common man."

The Antimason Party was formed to oppose the Masons, a secret society whose members included many important and wealthy people. (President Andrew Jackson was a Mason.) The disappearance of a man who slandered the Masons created a backlash against the society, which lead to the formation of the Antimasons.

When the Antimason Party dissolved in 1834, Seward and many of his colleagues became involved in another political group. Seward and his friend Thurlow Weed laid the groundwork for the new Whig Party. The support of ex-Antimasons allowed the Whigs to win more victories.

As the Whig Party broke up in 1855, Seward joined the new party with an old name—the Republicans. The Republican Party, with opposition to slavery at its core, sought to push the slavery issue to the front of American political debate.

Though Seward switched parties often, two things didn't change throughout his career: he was always involved in politics and he was always somewhere near the top.

A drawing attacking the Antimason Party, representing the Masons on the right side of the picture—with values such as science, sincerity, and equal rights—and the Antimasons on the left side, with negatives such as cowardice, slavery, and slander

Though less well known than Seward, Lincoln carried the Republican banner into the White House, winning the presidency in a four-man race. Seward was not left out in the cold, however. On December 8, 1860, the president-elect offered him the top cabinet position—secretary of the Department of State.

In the Cabinet

Seward was still determined to mold the United States into a world power. His dream was put on hold, however, when the Civil War erupted in April 1861. He hated the interruption. In the spring of 1861, when Spain annexed Santo Domingo (now the Dominican Republic) in the Caribbean, and France threatened Santo Domingo's neighbor, Haiti, Seward urged Lincoln to invoke the Monroe Doctrine and order the Europeans out of the hemisphere. If they refused, argued Seward, Lincoln should "convene Congress and declare war against them." The president, understandably more focused on domestic affairs, wisely refused; if the southern rebellion wasn't licked, there would be no United States to uphold the Monroe Doctrine.

Certain threatening rumors from across the Atlantic could not be ignored. France and Britain, with the world's leading textile industries, were the major consumers of Southern cotton. Because the U.S. naval blockade of Confederate ports cut off their cotton supply, word had it that France and Britain might intervene in the Civil War to restore their supply of the important raw material. That could doom the Northern war effort and with it the Union.

Seward handled this crisis calmly. "Would it be wise for her Majesty's government," he inquired of the British foreign minister, "to set a dangerous precedent, or provoke retaliation? . . . Has Great Britain no dependency, island, or province left exposed along the whole circle of her empire?" It certainly did, and in veiled language, Seward had just threatened the British province closest to

the United States—Canada. Loath to fight in North America again, Britain backed off.

Relations with Great Britain were still tense in November 1861 when sailors from the Union ship *San Jacinto* boarded the British vessel *Trent* off the coast of Cuba to arrest two Confederate diplomats en route to Great Britain. The British were furious. Seward well understood that they might retaliate for what seemed an affront to their national honor. Major seaports like New York, Boston, and Philadelphia, he warned Lincoln, were vulnerable to naval attack. Could the Union afford to withdraw troops from the field to defend these places? Seward had the men released on a technicality without ever agreeing that the U.S. had done anything wrong by arresting the so-called diplomats. Britain simply let the conflict end.

Seward managed to remove the threat of the French as well. When their minister suggested a relaxation of the blockade to allow partial resumption of cotton shipments,

The San Jacinto *(right) encounters the* Trent, *touching off a major diplomatic crisis between the United States and Britain.*

In the midst of dealing with foreign countries, Seward aided Lincoln in defeating the South. The two signed the Emancipation Proclamation in 1863, which ended slavery in the Confederate states.

Seward responded with tact and logic. It was true, he told the diplomat, that France had an interest in a speedy end to the war. He pointed out that a Union victory would benefit the French, as well, in that it would promote continued economic unity between France, Great Britain, and the U.S. But if the South were allowed to sell cotton, that would only make things harder on the North and prolong the conflict. The best move the French could make would be to stand aside and let the North crush the rebellion. Besides, Seward asked, did France really want to be seen helping a slave power survive? The French backed off.

As the ferocity of the Civil War escalated through 1862 to its climax at Gettysburg, Pennsylvania, in July 1863, Seward continued to contend with periodic grumbling from the French. Along the way, he issued a demand to the English that they cease sales of warships to the Confederacy.

Seward and Stanton

In 1862, Henry Seward encouraged the appointment of Edwin Stanton to the position of secretary of war. Seward had become friends with Stanton earlier in his career. Later in 1862, Seward contributed to the success of the War Department. Enlistments in the army had fallen off, and Seward helped develop a plan for governors in Union states to request more volunteers. Lincoln would then throw his support behind their call. Seward's plan roused the volunteering spirit again and about 200,000 men signed up, while another 100,000 pledged to enlist within the month. Seward's accomplishment meant that Lincoln did not have to start requiring men to join the military. Unfortunately, Lincoln would have to institute a draft the next year anyway.

Lincoln's cabinet included (clockwise from top) Secretary of State Seward, Secretary of the Navy Gideon Welles, Secretary of the Treasury Salmon P. Chase, and Secretary of War Edwin Stanton.

reparations: compensation paid by one nation to a nation it has done injury to or damaged in some way, usually during war

The Alabama *sinks the* Hatteras, *in January 1863. Seward wanted the British to pay reparations for the loss of the Union ship.*

One British vessel, sold to the rebels in July 1862 and renamed the *Alabama*, had sunk several Union ships. Seward's protests ended the sales, but forcing the British to pay reparations would have to wait until after the war.

For the rest of the war, the secretary of state kept his eye on the Europeans while continuing as Lincoln's closest advisor. The last fears of foreign involvement, as well as of Confederate victory, faded after the rebel defeat at Gettysburg. On April 9, 1865, the South surrendered. Seward lay in bed at the time, recovering from a carriage accident. He was still there on April 14 when John Wilkes Booth shot Lincoln at Ford's Theater. (The president would die the next day.) About the same time Booth fired his pistol, co-conspirator Lewis Powell sneaked into Seward's bedroom and stabbed the secretary. Seward's

Revenge for the "oppression" and defeat of the Confederacy motivated John Wilkes Booth (1838-1865) to attempt to kill Lincoln, Seward, and Vice President Johnson.

nurse, a soldier named George Robinson, wrestled the would-be assassin to the ground.

Seward was soon up and working as secretary of state again, this time under the new president, Andrew Johnson. Two major international problems remained from the war, the first involving the French. In the first months of 1862, a multinational force of British, Spanish, and French troops had occupied major ports in Mexico to reclaim money owed them by the Mexican government. Britain and Spain had withdrawn as soon as their claims were satisfied. France, driven by Emperor Napoleon III's long-held desire for a colony in the Western Hemisphere, remained. Seward now ordered the French out, in keeping with the Monroe Doctrine's "noncolonization" clause. Napoleon had no favorable options. His puppet ruler in Mexico, Ferdinand Maximilian, was 6,000 miles from France, a dangerously long supply line even for today's armies. Underscoring the point, U.S. general Ulysses S. Grant was quietly amassing 50,000 battle-hardened troops on

Ferdinand Maximilian (1832-1867) was executed by Mexican soldiers when he tried to remain emperor after the French troops had left.

arbitration: a means of solving a conflict between two or more nations in which the differences are presented to an impartial court

tribunal: a judicial court or a committee appointed to resolve a dispute

Mexico's northern border. Napoleon III gave in to the inevitability of U.S. dominance in the Western Hemisphere and withdrew his troops.

Convincing the British to pay reparations for the *Alabama* destruction, Seward's second problem, would be trickier. In fact, he never collected a dime. His success came in negotiating the Treaty of Washington, eventually signed in May 1871. The treaty marked a major shift for the better in Anglo-American relations by establishing arbitration instead of war as a means of settling major differences. In August 1872, an international tribunal found the British liable for $15 million in damages caused by the *Alabama* and its two sister ships. Other disputes, like those centering on borders and fishing rights in the Pacific Northwest, were settled in like manner later in the year. Peaceful resolution of conflicts between the two nations became the norm.

Of course, the British didn't just wake up one day and decide never to fight the United States again. In 1867, Seward had purchased Alaska from Russia. Derided by critics as "Seward's Icebox," Alaska nevertheless was a valuable resource for gold, and its coastal waters teemed with fish. Most attractive to Seward, however, was Alaska's geographic position; together with the lower United States, it formed a vise around Canada. Fearful of losing Canada in the event of war, Great Britain agreed to arbitrate future disagreements.

The purchase of Alaska was part of Seward's dream of peaceful American dominance of the Western Hemisphere.

This political cartoon depicts Seward's purchase of Alaska as balm for Andrew Johnson's "sore spot." Some newspapers criticized the Alaska purchase as an attempt to cover up the failures of the Johnson administration at home (especially Reconstruction, the federal government's effort to rebuild the defeated South in accordance with U.S. law).

He also hoped to acquire islands for use as navy outposts to guard the ocean approaches to a future canal across Central America, or as coaling stations for merchant and naval ships navigating the trade route to Asia. In 1867, Seward tried to buy the Dutch West Indies, but the deal fell through. (The U.S. did acquire some of the islands—today's Virgin Islands—in 1917.) An attempt to annex Hawaii the following year also misfired. (Future president William McKinley would annex Hawaii in 1898.) Seward did acquire tiny Brooks Island in the Pacific, but most Americans wouldn't even know it existed until 1942. That year, Brooks, known as Midway since 1903, was the site of the great U.S. Navy victory over the Japanese fleet that marked the beginning of the end for Japan in World War II.

The State Department in Washington, D.C., as it looked in 1866 when William Seward was secretary of state.

Before leaving office, Seward looked into buying Greenland and Iceland—a rather transparent attempt to encircle Canada and force it to join the Union. With little support from the American public, the deal died. (The United States was still reeling financially from the Civil War, causing many to question America's immediate need for more land.) Seward also sought Spain's possessions of Cuba and Puerto Rico and newly independent (since 1865) Santo Domingo and Haiti. Congressional indifference ended the pursuit. Senators were interested when Seward tried to buy the Colombian province of Panama, where the secretary envisioned a canal connecting the Atlantic and Pacific Oceans. The transfer failed, however, when the Colombians backed out. (The Panama Canal would open in 1914.) There things stood as Seward retired in March 1869.

Looking Forward

Three and a half years later, on October 10, 1872, William Henry Seward died. As one historian noted, Seward's tenure as secretary of state was marked by blatant opportunism. Seward took every opportunity short of war to achieve his vision of the United States dominating the Western Hemisphere and leading the world. Although he failed to achieve world leadership for the United States during his lifetime, Seward laid the foundation for future greatness by helping Lincoln maintain the Union and by working to shape friendlier Anglo-American relations.

As tensions eased between Great Britain and the United States, the greatest threat to the U.S. in the Western Hemisphere disappeared. Yet the Royal Navy remained behind to protect Britain's dwindling hemispheric interests—Canada and other colonies in the Caribbean and Latin America—from European rivals. Thanks to its location, the United States fell under this naval shield. Thus freed from spending great sums on defense, the U.S. focused instead on expanding its power through increased trade and the acquisition of territory.

JOHN MILTON HAY

Great Power Diplomacy

Henry Seward was young John Hay's real mentor in the Lincoln administration. True, Hay came to love Abraham Lincoln as a father, but it was Seward's vision for U.S. greatness that captured Hay's imagination. He even honored the secretary in a poem:

> Thy fame will broaden through the centuries;
> As, storm and billowy tumult overpast,
> The moon rules calmly o'er the conquered seas.

Seward's dream was for the United States to reign someday as the democratic leader of the world, its benevolence predominant in the Western Hemisphere, its peaceful influence global. When Seward died in 1872, his vision passed to Hay, who would give it life.

The Formative Years

John Milton Hay, fourth of six children, was born in Salem, Indiana, on October 8, 1838. John was the weakest brother, but physical shortcoming was offset by exceptional intelligence. Charles and Helen Hay did all they could to provide their gifted son with a first-rate education.

By his 12th birthday, John could speak German and read Latin and Greek. He had also taken the first step—although unknowingly—toward his future career. His uncle, Milton Hay of Pittsfield, Illinois, had agreed to

With his famous Open Door Notes, John Milton Hay (1838-1905) managed to keep China open for free trade and set a precedent of cooperation among nations.

board his nephew so John could attend the local school. A lawyer, Milton had studied law years earlier under Abraham Lincoln. The two had developed a friendship that Milton later used to land his nephew a job in the Lincoln administration.

In the spring of 1852, John and his brother Augustus entered Illinois State University in nearby Springfield. John excelled, and in 1855 he moved to Providence, Rhode Island, to enroll in prestigious Brown University. At graduation in 1858, John stood first in his class, leading classmates to joke that he could "put his book under his pillow and [have] the contents thereof absorbed and digested by morning." Learning wasn't really that easy, even for John Hay. He read and studied constantly. In what spare time he could muster, he wrote poetry.

Although John returned to Illinois in 1858 to eventually study law with Milton, he was not especially drawn to a legal career. He refused to seek riches or power for their own sake. At Brown, he had written a poem about his dream of going forth

> ... to learn of love and truth,
> From Nature smiling in eternal youth;
> To ponder long on infinite wealth and power,
> Squandered to deck with gold one wayside flower ...

True wealth and power, in John's view, was to be found in the quest for love and truth. As the decade of the 1850s faded, the young poet looked in vain for such a righteous quest. Then came Abraham Lincoln and the Civil War.

Actually, Hay was slow to recognize that saving the Union could be the quest he sought. That's probably because Lincoln, at least initially, was such an unlikely savior. He seemed to lack confidence and ability. As the war progressed, however, Hay came to regard the president with great respect, even to believe "the hand of God placed him where he is." By the time Hay wrote this of Lincoln in August 1863, the president had become a competent war

John Hay was 22 when the Civil War began in 1860. The young Hay admired President Abraham Lincoln and Secretary of State Henry Seward for their leadership during the war years.

leader. But Hay's admiration went beyond the president's command abilities. Lincoln was the undeniable soul of the Union, the glue holding it together. And the style of government of the United States, despite its faults, was still "the sole hope of a sick world." To Hay, that made the president, mistakes and all, "the greatest character since Christ."

While Hay saw Lincoln as the man to point the world toward political salvation, he eventually recognized Secretary of State Henry Seward as the journey's day-to-day guide. It would fall to Seward to hammer out the treaties and purchase the territory that would make the United States the powerful republican model Lincoln foresaw.

Hay determined to help Seward in any way possible. He accepted appointment in March 1865 as secretary to the United States legation (a diplomatic establishment ranking lower than an embassy) in Paris, France. There

embassy: a diplomatic establishment in a foreign country in which an ambassador works to conduct relations with that country

Hay remained until February 1867, when he returned to the United States to seek another office. He got what he wanted, and in June he traveled to Vienna, Austria, to serve as charge d'affaires (the diplomat who temporarily heads a legation that is waiting for a replacement minister). When the Vienna assignment ended in 1868, Hay again served as secretary, this time to the U.S. minister in Madrid, Spain.

Although Hay never wavered in his conviction that republicanism was the wave of the future, he had lost much of his earlier spiritual zeal by September 1870. Part of the reason was that Horace Greeley, famed editor of the *New York Tribune*, had offered Hay a job—the type of writing position Hay had yearned for since his days at Brown. Another factor was that Hay, after five years abroad, wanted to settle down in one place for a while. It's possible, too, that he felt great frustration after years of holding low-ranking positions under the real policymakers. Whatever the case, Hay abandoned his crusade and left the State Department.

Horace Greeley (1811-1872) founded the New York Tribune *in 1841 and worked as its chief editor. He was one of six presidential candidates in the 1872 election. He died a few weeks after the election—but before his 66 electors voted. In the electoral balloting, 63 of Greeley's votes were divided among four other candidates. Ulysses S. Grant was reelected president.*

For the next several years, he wrote editorials and articles about international relations for the *Tribune*. Hay contributed even after he moved to Ohio with his new wife, Clara Stone, whom he had married in February 1874. By then his interests had begun to shift yet again—this time to the world of business. Clara's father, Amasa Stone, was a wealthy industrialist and banker who saw in John Hay someone capable of managing his investments. Hay agreed to help Stone.

It wasn't long before Hay felt his life drifting away from any real meaning. Deciding to return to government work, Hay accepted a position as assistant secretary of state in November 1879. The job gave him little satisfaction, since it was geared toward administration rather than policymaking. Hay resigned in March 1881.

During the next 17 years, he wrote political articles and cowrote a massive 10-volume biography of Lincoln. When Amasa Stone died in 1883 and left John and Clara $3.5 million, Hay was suddenly very rich. In none of this did he find contentment. When asked in 1892 how he and his family were doing, Hay replied, "We live a languid, vegetable life. Everybody asks me—'What do you do?' and the question leaves me speechless." What he wanted was to recapture the vision that had swept him along in 1861. Only this time around, Hay wanted to lead the diplomatic mission to save the world—just like his idol, Henry Seward.

William McKinley's election to the presidency in 1896 saved John Hay. In his campaign as the Republican candidate for president, McKinley had called for a strong navy capable of enforcing the Monroe Doctrine; control over Hawaii and several islands in the Caribbean; and "the ultimate union of all English-speaking parts of the continent by the free consent of its inhabitants." With this program, the U.S. would dominate the Western Hemisphere and exercise a great deal of global power. It was as if Seward himself had written the Republican Party platform. When

William McKinley (1843-1901), the 25th president of the United States, was a staunch protectionist who supported higher tariffs on imports.

McKinley offered Hay the ambassadorship to Great Britain in March 1897—the most prestigious overseas U.S. posting—Hay rightly saw it as the steppingstone to the office of secretary of state and accepted immediately.

Ambassador Hay arrived in London in April. Hay, who was popular in Britain for his biography of Lincoln, was fond of the British and their culture. Assistant Secretary of the Navy Theodore Roosevelt even complained that Hay was "more English than the English" and, therefore, "could not be trusted" to stand up for the United States. Such talk was rubbish, in Hay's opinion. The time for antagonizing Great Britain was past. If the U.S. was ever going to join the ranks of world leaders, it could choose no better model than the greatest empire the world had ever seen.

Hay's admiration of the British stemmed in part from his sympathy with "Anglo-Saxonism." A popular movement at the time, Anglo-Saxonism placed white, English-speaking peoples at the top of an imaginary social ladder. Their greatest art, Anglo-Saxonists believed, was government. It was their duty to "guide" nonwhite peoples until they could responsibly govern themselves. Hay believed the United States and Great Britain were "joint ministers of the same sacred mission of liberty and progress," whose growing friendship was "a necessity of civilization." Nurturing the Anglo-American relationship thus became Hay's top priority.

The move paid off during America's war with Spain in 1898. During the previous year, President McKinley had been trying to end a bloody rebellion on the Spanish island of Cuba. In January 1898, he ordered the battleship *Maine* into Havana harbor, hoping to intimidate the Spanish into ending their slaughter of nationalist Cubans. The Spanish ignored the maneuver. Their minister in Washington even called McKinley "weak" and a "would-be politician." On February 15, a mysterious explosion destroyed the *Maine*, killing 266 sailors. The situation only became worse from there, and Congress declared war on April 19.

The USS Maine, *sunk in Havana harbor*

American troops stationed in the Philippines at Manila during the Spanish-American War

From Britain, Hay was able to report that his host was "the only European country whose sympathies are not openly against us." That was good news; British neutrality made European intervention on Spain's behalf unlikely. But the British weren't just neutral, they were actively aiding the Americans. They gave Hay Spanish diplomatic messages that had been intercepted, denied coal to the Spanish fleet while giving it to U.S. Navy vessels, and relayed messages from American warships to Washington. With no need to guard its "Atlantic flank," the United States easily defeated Spain, taking Cuba and nearby Puerto Rico, as well as the Philippine Islands in the Pacific. From start to speedy finish four months later, the affair was, in Hay's now-famous opinion, a "splendid little war."

Suddenly, with control of the Caribbean and a strong presence in the Pacific—Congress had also annexed Hawaii during the war—the United States was as great a power as any in Europe. As Hay had predicted years earlier in his poetic tribute to Henry Seward, the moon finally ruled over seas conquered by American might.

By strengthening the Anglo-American bond, Hay had done his part. "In the long list of famous American Ministers in London," wrote Henry Adams, "none could have given the work quite the completeness, the harmony, the perfect ease of Hay." Presumably Adams considered his own grandfather, John Quincy Adams, when he wrote these words. McKinley approved of Hay's performance, as well. In the aftermath of the war, he nominated the veteran diplomat to lead the State Department. Hay assumed office on September 30, 1898.

The U.S. flag is raised in Hawaii after annexation in 1898. In 1893, native Hawaiian rulers had been overthrown in a revolt led by American sugar growers. The new government requested annexation to the United States, but President Grover Cleveland refused, believing that the government did not have the support of the Hawaiian people. President McKinley reversed this decision, and the Hawaiian Islands became a U.S. territory.

In the Cabinet

Despite a knack for diplomacy, Hay was limited in what he could achieve of his dream for American greatness. The problem was, while Americans welcomed world power, they continued to shun involvement in foreign wars or alliances of any kind. The two attitudes have never mixed well.

Hay's first test was brewing even as he returned from Britain in the late summer of 1898. France and Germany had begun pressuring the African nation of Liberia to grant special trade privileges that would give them an economic edge over everyone else. Hay immediately objected. Commercial concessions were usually a first step toward formal annexation and colonization. The United States could never allow that. For one thing, Liberia had been founded in 1821 by Americans as a haven for former slaves and even had a government modeled on that of the United States. Second, the U.S. Navy hoped to place a coaling station there. Even though the Monroe Doctrine had never been meant to extend to Africa, Hay nonetheless believed that to allow the African republic to fall into the hands of the Europeans would threaten the security of the United States.

With no military might of his own to back his diplomacy, Hay turned to Great Britain. He convinced the British to call for free trade and political independence for Liberia. The United States did the same. (This situation is a good example of the limitations Hay faced. He could not issue the call jointly with the British—that would have seemed too much like an alliance and would never have gained the American public's approval. He and the British issued separate but concurrent statements instead.) With the subtle threat of British military might lurking in the background, France and Germany agreed to Hay's policy of free trade in Liberia.

Hay now shifted his championship of free trade eastward. Improving trade with the Far East had been a major American goal since Daniel Webster headed the State

Department in the early 1840s. Much had been achieved since then: Japan had been opened to U.S. merchants in the 1850s, and islands had been acquired along the trade route to serve as coaling stations for American ships. Now the United States faced the prospect of losing access to the potentially lucrative Chinese market to Japan and the European powers—Britain, France, Italy, Russia, and Germany. By April 1899, these countries had carved China into exclusive trade zones. Hay had to convince everyone involved to respect the concept of free trade.

Hay responded calmly with two diplomatic messages known as the Open Door Notes. The first was sent in September 1899 and asked simply that all nations work to ensure free trade (nicknamed the "open door"). This included the establishment of equal tariff, railroad, and harbor rates in their spheres. Hay made no threat of military force; he didn't have the American public's support. Besides, any threat could inflame the already tense situation.

John Hay and his younger son, Clarence Leonard Hay

★ ★

Daniel Webster: The Expansion of Trade

Improving trade with the Far East became a major goal of U.S. diplomats in the 1840s because of the large, unapproached markets there. Daniel Webster, secretary of state from 1841 to 1843 and again from 1850 to 1852, envisioned a commercial "chain" running westward from the United States, through the Hawaiian Islands and Japan, to a final linkup with China.

Webster secured the initial link in late 1842. In response to European expansion that threatened U.S. access to the Hawaiian Islands, an important way station to Asia, the secretary crafted a policy statement that President John Tyler delivered in December. Soon dubbed the Tyler Doctrine, it proclaimed the importance of Hawaii (then called the Sandwich Islands) to America's continued prosperity and warned that any attempt "by another power . . . to take possession of the islands, colonize them, and subvert the native government" would be seen by the United States as an unfriendly act.

Webster's next move was to secure access to Chinese ports for American merchants. This was the easternmost link in the chain. Webster knew most of the wealthiest merchants personally, and they believed that one day the Chinese market would be America's biggest. At the time, U.S. ships could anchor in only one port. The British, in contrast, had just gained entrance to their sixth. In May 1843, Webster sent

Daniel Webster (1782-1852) was a famous U.S. statesman who served as a lawyer arguing before the Supreme Court, as a congressman and senator, and as secretary of state.

diplomats to China (America's first to that empire) to negotiate equal access for U.S. ships. The successful outcome was the Treaty of Wanghia, signed the following year. Webster left office, satisfied that his chain to the Far East was complete.

The rapid rise of the steamship quickly changed this. Sailing ships had dominated the oceans during Webster's first term in the State Department. By 1850, however, steam engines were showing enough promise that Webster

56

could plainly see that they would soon replace sails. The primitive engines of the day burned a lot of coal, however, and the returning secretary of state was forced to add an additional link in his chain, one that provided a fueling station for America's steamers.

Fortunately, the islands of Japan, conveniently astride the U.S. trade route to China, had coal. Unfortunately, Japan was a closed society and had been since 1638. Webster pressed ahead anyway. He sent Commodore Matthew Perry to open diplomatic relations with the mysterious islands. Perry succeeded in 1853, signing a treaty that opened Japan to the world and ensured access to coal for American ships. Daniel Webster never saw the great chain completed; he had died the previous year.

Daniel Webster addresses the U.S. Senate in 1850.

★ ★

British troops entering Peking, China, to put down the Boxer Rebellion in 1900. The Boxers were members of a secret society dedicated to driving all foreigners and foreign customs out of China. "Boxers" was a derogatory term derived from the society's Chinese name, which meant "Righteous and Harmonious Fists."

The recipients of the note responded favorably, but all expressed reservations. This was a problem. If just one nation ignored Hay's proposed guidelines, the rest probably would, too. Hay and the United States would look foolish, and the problem would continue to fester. The clever secretary avoided this by simply announcing in March 1900 that everyone had accepted the note. Hay's exaggeration produced the desired result: everyone thought everyone else was on board, so no one jumped ship.

Four months later, a new crisis forced Hay to issue a second note. Chinese nationalists, called Boxers, had murdered several western diplomats in what has been termed the Boxer Rebellion. A European force of 19,000 soldiers, joined by 5,000 Americans, rushed to the scene. Fearing a complete takeover of China by the Europeans, Hay stressed in his second note that it was U.S. policy to seek a peaceful solution that "may bring about permanent safety and peace to China," that would preserve China as a "territorial and administrative entity," and that would "safeguard for the world the principle of equal and impartial trade with all parts of the Chinese Empire."

The secretary's second message reached much further than the first. For one thing, it sought to extend free trade to all parts of China, not just to those currently under foreign domination. Furthermore, the second note mentioned for the first time the U.S. desire to preserve China as a nation. Like Seward and Adams before him, Hay dreamed of building the United States into a great moral power, a republican model for the world. Ensuring the existence of a weak country fit perfectly into his plan.

When William McKinley was assassinated in 1901, Theodore Roosevelt (back center) became president and inherited his cabinet, including John Hay (left and forward of Roosevelt.)

What effect the second note had on Japanese and European behavior is difficult to gauge. Hay certainly had no public mandate to force their compliance. Americans were still reluctant to believe that their nation's security—its ability to survive and prosper—required fighting on foreign soil. What the Open Door Policy did accomplish was to push the United States further away from its tradition of shunning European politics.

Looking Forward

Besides fostering good relations with Great Britain and expanding American interests to include the Far East, Hay is remembered for the treaty he negotiated with British ambassador Julian Pauncefote, which authorized the United States to build, own, and operate a canal through Central America. The Hay-Pauncefote agreement of November 1901 helped to clear the way for the eventual

The construction of the Panama Canal, begun in 1904, was a major engineering feat that took 10 years to complete. In November 1909, work on the canal was delayed by a mudslide that buried trains and steam shovels.

opening of the Panama Canal in 1914. Before the canal's construction, merchant ships steaming from New York to San Francisco Bay had to round the tip of South America, a journey of some 13,600 miles. The distance dropped to 5,300 miles with the shortcut through Central America. The canal greatly improved the U.S. Navy's ability to safeguard "America's" hemisphere.

Although his health began to fail in 1903, Hay continued to lead the State Department until his death on July 1, 1905. It had taken more than three decades, but he had finally recaptured the vision of U.S. greatness expressed by Abraham Lincoln and Henry Seward.

This photograph, taken in July 1910, shows the construction of the Upper Gatun Locks, one of six pairs of locks on the Panama Canal.

The Hay-Pauncefote Treaty replaced the Clayton-Bulwer Treaty, which had stated that neither the U.S. nor Britain would seek or maintain exclusive rights to any canal built across Central America.

$\star \ \star \ 4 \ \star \ \star$

CHARLES EVANS HUGHES

Last Gasp for Isolationism

Little Charles Hughes, barely three, would never forget "the cry of anguish" when his father learned of Abraham Lincoln's assassination. Even though David Hughes had been in the United States only 10 years, Charles remembered that his father was "so completely American and my upbringing so dominated by American thought, that I never had any sense of being identified with his family abroad [in Wales]." David was deeply committed to something President Lincoln had been trying to build—a republic based on truth and justice that would be a model for the world.

When he took the reins of U.S. foreign policy in 1921, Charles Evans Hughes accepted Lincoln's mission, but cautiously. It was all right for the United States to act as a republican example. But until the day when other nations based their foreign policies on reason instead of brute force, the United States had to resist political and military entanglement.

The Formative Years

On April 11, 1862, Charles Evans Hughes was born in the town of Glens Falls, New York. David and Mary Hughes stressed service to God above all else to their only child. As the boy grew, he developed his parents' sense of duty and

Secretary of State Charles Evans Hughes (1862-1948) supported a more internationalist policy than most of his predecessors, but he also believed that changes in policy should be made slowly and should always reflect public opinion.

discipline. By the age of four, he could read; by five, he could recite much of the Bible's New Testament. When Mary enrolled Charles in school at age nine, he shot to the top of the class.

Charles graduated from high school second in his class in 1875. He was 13 years old. Two years at New York's Madison University (now Colgate) followed. But the school's rural setting bored him, so in 1878 Charles transferred to Brown University in Providence, Rhode Island.

There Hughes developed his political philosophy. From Professor Ezekiel Robinson he heard the view that reason was a gift from God to be used to solve humanity's problems. Professor J. Lewis Diman developed the idea further, stressing that throughout history people had been evolving intellectually and morally. In the context of international relations, Diman argued that among peoples who once relied solely on brute force to settle disputes, "a code of international ethics has been developed." Diman cautioned that changes in government and law should be made slowly. When Hughes left Brown upon graduating in the spring of 1881, he took with him the belief in reason's power to solve problems and the conviction that national progress could be achieved only slowly and with public support.

In the autumn of 1882, Hughes entered Columbia Law School in New York City. He finished 18 months later at the top of his class. After passing the bar exam (the licensing test for lawyers) with a near-perfect score, 22-year-old Hughes began what would become a long and successful career. He married Antoinette Carter in December 1888 and settled into a comfortable, satisfying life. Any dreams of changing the world that he might have had at Brown seemed to fade over the next several years.

That began to change in the spring of 1905. Hughes accepted a spot on a state legislative committee investigating unusually high gas and electricity rates in New York City. He found he loved the work. In fact, so zealous was

Hughes at rooting out corruption that in 1906, leading Republicans nominated him for governor just to keep him from uncovering possible wrongdoing by their national committee. The tactic worked; watchdog Hughes won the election and left for the governor's mansion.

New Yorkers quickly found Hughes to be strong-willed in his support for more government regulation. He hounded state legislators until they passed safety measures for railway workers and firefighters, laws for eight-hour workdays, and guarantees to workers of continued pay in case of injury. When lawmakers resisted Hughes, as they did when he tried to outlaw racetrack gambling, the governor made speeches to the people of New York in an attempt to get their support. Ultimately, he believed, "no remedy is possible which does not have its roots in general sentiment. . . ." The maneuver worked and Hughes got his law. The people spoke favorably again in November 1908 when they awarded Hughes a second two-year term as governor.

Charles Evans Hughes during one of his terms as governor of New York

Hughes achieved great influence over the next 12 years. When his second term as governor ended in 1910, President William Howard Taft appointed him to the U.S. Supreme Court. Then, in 1916, the Republicans nominated Hughes for president. War had been raging in Europe since the summer of 1914. The incumbent president, Woodrow Wilson, hoped to prevent future conflicts by enrolling all nations in a postwar federation. Hughes disliked the idea. He didn't mind international involvement, but he thought the "league of nations" idea was too radical. Hughes ran an honorable race, but, for once, success deserted him. He lost by only 591,000 votes, a mere sliver of the more than 17,600,000 cast.

Out of government for the next four years, Hughes watched drastic changes shake the world. The "Great War" (World War I) raged in Europe, with Britain, Russia, France, and Italy fighting against the Central Powers of

A determined campaigner for his fellow Republicans, Charles Evans Hughes addresses a rural Minnesota audience on behalf of William Howard Taft during the 1908 presidential race.

The 28th president of the United States, Woodrow Wilson (1856-1924), led the nation into World War 1 during his second term in office. Wilson hoped that the League of Nations would help prevent future wars, but Americans were not willing to join the international organization.

Germany, Austria-Hungary, and Turkey, who were trying to expand across the continent. In the first two years of the war, the economy of the United States became increasingly dependent on the Allies, as American sales of foodstuffs and munitions to these countries quadrupled in volume. Although 116,000 Americans died after the U.S. joined the Allies in April 1917, the total paled in comparison to Europe's losses—a total of 10 million dead and the continent left in ruins when the war ended in November 1918. Japan spent the war expanding its power, driving the Germans out of China and off several Pacific islands. By the war's end, Japan was dominant in the Far East.

Despite Europe's upheaval and the alarming growth of Japanese power in Asia, Americans wanted nothing more

Warren Harding (1865-1923) promised a return to the traditional foreign policy of expanding trade while avoiding any international commitments that could lead to war.

to do with the world. They rejected Wilson's call to join the League of Nations. Most Americans had been willing to fight authoritarian German rule, but now, to entangle the nation indefinitely in the affairs of Europe and Asia—that was simply asking too much. They elected Warren G. Harding president in November 1920. On December 10, Harding, in turn, selected a secretary of state whose beliefs largely mirrored his own—Charles Evans Hughes.

In the Cabinet

Hughes took office with a concrete plan to achieve the tranquil global landscape necessary for American prosperity. He thought that, to some extent, action out of self-interest was necessary for human development, but that it was more important for individual goals to be subordinated to the "common welfare." The League of Nations seemed to demand just that. For instance, the League treaty required all members to "respect and preserve as against external aggression the territorial integrity and existing political independence" of all other members. In other words, if one nation attacked another, then everyone else was expected to join in repelling the aggressor.

While Hughes agreed with the general idea of the League, he still believed that change had to come slowly, through changing public opinion. The League of Nations was too radical a change, and the American public would never support that much U.S. involvement in world affairs all at once, according to Hughes.

Hughes wanted to slow the whole process down. The most practical approach, he thought, would be to develop international laws gradually, through arbitration and treaty negotiations. In Hughes's view, such reasonable discussion and settlement would satisfy the participants enough so that there would be no need for force. Any disputes could be settled through judgments from either an international court of law or from an impartial mediator, such as a respected head of state. Since his days at Brown,

Hughes had believed in the evolution of humanity toward more rational and reasonable interaction. It was time to take another step.

Hughes focused first on his own country. He urged that the United States join the Permanent Court of International Justice, or World Court, at The Hague, Netherlands. Its judges were picked by members of the League of Nations, so they were expected to be impartial. And their expertise in international law went without saying. But the U.S. Senate—which had to approve any treaty of membership—balked. Senators wanted no connection to the League of Nations. Hughes suggested certain amendments to the treaty ensuring that the League exercised no power over the United States. Still he failed. When the Senate finally voted on membership in the Court in January 1936, they did not reach the two-thirds majority needed to approve the membership.

Now administered by the United Nations (UN), the World Court still settles disputes between member countries. Nations that are not part of the UN may also submit disputes to the court under certain conditions. The court is made up of 15 judges from different countries.

Delegates met in Washington, D.C., on November 11, 1921, for a naval disarmament conference, out of which came the Five-Power Treaty.

While pressing for U.S. involvement in a mechanism to resolve disputes peacefully, Hughes took what steps he could to lessen the chance for war. The threat was growing daily. Japan, Great Britain, and the United States were locked in a naval arms race. Japan, the third strongest maritime power, was investing one-third of its entire budget into ship construction, while the U.S. was spending unprecedented sums to improve its second-ranked navy. The British fleet was desperately seeking funds to maintain its position at the top. To Hughes, enormous outlays for national defense made no sense. Instead of fostering security, huge militaries actually achieved the opposite by increasing tensions. To reverse the situation, Hughes negotiated the world's first disarmament pact—the Five-Power Treaty of 1922.

From the first moments of the disarmament conference held in Washington between November 1921 and February 1922, Hughes took charge. To the representatives of the four other major sea powers—Great Britain, Japan, France, and Italy—Hughes made a staggering announcement. The United States would voluntarily scuttle 30 capital ships (the heaviest warships—battleships and battle cruisers). The American secretary then went around the table and slashed navies as the other foreign ministers stared in amazement. The Royal Navy would scrap 19 ships, the Japanese, 17, and so on. In the first half-hour, a British observer noted, Hughes destroyed more ships "than all the admirals of the world have sunk in a cycle of centuries."

Charles Evans Hughes (second from right) with other delegates to the conference on arms limitation

Charles Evans Hughes with Frank B. Kellogg (1856-1937), his successor as secretary of state

To appreciate Hughes's gesture fully, consider that in the 1920s the primary means of deterring an invasion for a nation bordering the sea was its navy. The seagoing nation also depended on its navy to protect its merchant shipping, its sources of raw materials, and its access to commercial markets. In short, coastal nations could not be major powers without great navies; they might not even be able to remain independent at all. And what made navies great? Heavy warships. Hughes, by suggesting that the five major seapowers slash their capital ships, was asking that they willingly give up their main source of military and economic power. This might have made as little sense as anything the League was asking them to do, but Hughes thought he could push the thing through if everyone agreed to the plan. That way, no one nation would gain the advantage.

Remarkably, everyone did agree, with the strongest powers of Great Britain, the United States, and Japan giving up a total of 66 capital ships. Furthermore, the five powers agreed not to build any capital ships for 10 years. Finally, they decided on a ratio of naval power that fixed the Royal Navy and the U.S. Navy at the top, the Japanese below them, and the French and Italian fleets in the third spot. Hughes had won an extraordinary victory.

Unfortunately, he won it for Japan. True, the treaty permitted the United States to maintain a navy that was second to none. However, because of the number of ships

Hughes with his wife, Antoinette Carter, whom he married on December 5, 1888

allotted Japan, the U.S. would still be hard pressed to stop the Japanese should the two find themselves on opposite sides in a world war. That's because the U.S. Navy would have to fight in two oceans (the Atlantic as well as the Pacific) while the Japanese fleet could concentrate its power in the Pacific alone.

Still another shortcoming of the treaty was a clause prohibiting the United States, Great Britain, and Japan from further fortifying their territorial possessions in the Pacific. The Japanese, who feared a reinforced American military presence in the Philippines, had insisted on this point. Japan's anxiety was understandable; a U.S. Navy strong enough to guarantee the security of the Philippines would be a force capable of blockading the Japanese islands. Unfortunately, because they were left inadequately defended, American and British possessions in the Pacific later became easy targets for Japanese conquest.

Looking Forward

Truth be told, Hughes had little faith that arms limitation would last. "Competitive armament is the outward sign of an inward distrust," he wrote in 1926, "and will go on until confidence replaces fear and suspicion." While it was his hope that someday nations would turn to the World Court to resolve disputes instead of resorting to military force, he knew it would take time for people's attitudes to evolve.

Hughes didn't insist on an enforcement clause in the Five-Power Treaty for this reason. Such enforcement would have required the United States to act automatically and in unison with others. Hughes refused to commit the U.S. to a certain course of action before a crisis developed. The United States, he insisted a month before leaving the State Department in March 1925, had to remain free "to follow the dictates of reason" and "to take the action approved by an enlightened people." In other words, the United States would interact with the rest of the world, but on its terms and in its best interest.

Hughes left office amid showers of praise. "Probably not since John Quincy Adams have we had a more capable director of our foreign affairs," claimed one publication. The accolades were understandable. Hughes had championed the rule of law and reason, he had forced arms reduction on the strongest nations, and his Five-Power Treaty assured the U.S. Navy of parity with the mighty British fleet. Best of all, he had done it all without surrendering U.S. freedom of action.

After leaving office, Hughes accepted appointment to the Permanent Court of Arbitration at The Hague, Netherlands, in 1926. Three years later, in May 1929, he took a seat on the bench of the World Court, also at The Hague. From there Hughes moved for a second time to the United States Supreme Court in February 1930, where he served as chief justice until his retirement in 1941. Charles Evans Hughes died on August 27, 1948.

Charles Evans Hughes in his robes as chief justice of the United States Supreme Court

★ ★ 5 ★ ★

DEAN GOODERHAM ACHESON

The Truman Doctrine and Internationalism

In late 1939, as the Japanese were gobbling up territory in the Far East and the Germans were mopping up after crushing Poland, Dean Acheson discussed the threat to the U.S. before a Yale University audience. The real danger for the United States was not sudden death by conquest, he pointed out, but rather slow strangulation from restricted trade and diminished supplies of raw materials. The British were no longer rich enough to finance the "means of production of wealth in other countries" or strong enough to "guarantee security of life and [commercial] investment in distant parts of the earth." If the United States stood by and did nothing, forces hostile to democracy and free trade—like the Germans and the Japanese—would assume Great Britain's traditional leadership role.

What did Acheson suggest the United States do? "I think it is clear," he said, "that with a nation, as with a boxer, one of the greatest assurances of safety is to add reach to our power." He meant military power. Acheson thought that Americans should support a major buildup of their army and navy, and that they should support increased arms shipments to those nations battling Germany and Japan. But Acheson also wanted the United States to increase its economic reach. Once the authoritarian threat

Dean Acheson (1893-1971) wrote the Truman Doctrine, which declared that the U.S. would support and defend the freedom of people around the world.

was vanquished, it would be up to the United States to rebuild the world's productive capability and to ensure free trade among nations. In short, for the U.S. to be truly secure, it would have to assume leadership of the world.

The Formative Years

Dean Gooderham Acheson, the first son of Edward and Eleanor (Gooderham) Acheson, was born on April 11, 1893, in Middletown, Connecticut. As Dean recalled, it was a safe and quiet place to live. How different his world would eventually become.

Growing up, Dean acquired certain traits from his parents. Eleanor, daughter of a prosperous family, spoke her mind and usually dominated any crowd. (And she could drop a squirrel with a single blast from the shotgun she kept behind the front door!) Edward, more reserved, was no less a force in Dean's life. He was a decorated veteran of the Canadian military and a dedicated Christian minister. A detached and stoical man, he rarely wavered in his personal discipline.

Dean took more after his mother in his early years. Independent and rebellious, the boy usually stayed in trouble at the nearby boarding school he attended after his ninth birthday. When in 1905 he entered the prestigious Groton School near Boston, Massachusetts, his behavior didn't improve much. In a structured environment where "obedience and conformity were commended," young Acheson was bound to disappoint. He graduated dead last in his class in 1911 with a *D* average.

His next stop was Yale University, which he attended from 1911 to 1915. Again, most of Dean's time was spent goofing off. All that mattered to him were stylish clothes, a nice car, and coaching the rowing team—from which he was fired early on, after one particularly dreadful defeat. Even Dean admitted years later that he wasted the Yale years "learning things that were meaningless."

Many young men in the early 1900s who attended prestigious preparatory schools were subsequently accepted by a prestigious college such as Harvard or Yale—often regardless of past performance.

Then came Harvard Law School in the autumn of 1915, the turning point in Acheson's life. Something in him clicked when he met Professor Felix Frankfurter, a future justice of the U.S. Supreme Court. Frankfurter relished gathering statistics to support or dispute federal legislation. He thought the law derived from facts and that law books could provide no answers to legal issues. Frankfurter passed his love of activism and learning on to Acheson, who came to realize that excellence did count, that "a sloppy try wasn't enough." Something else Frankfurter taught Acheson was to approach each problem with an open mind and never to be afraid to apply new and untried solutions.

Dean Acheson with Felix Frankfurter, his former professor

Supreme Court Justices (from left) Harlan Stone, Oliver Wendell Holmes, and Louis Brandeis. Holmes and Brandeis were both role models for Dean Acheson.

Acheson had found his groove. After graduating fifth in his class from Harvard in June 1918, he met two other men who became major influences on him. One was Louis Brandeis, a justice on the U.S. Supreme Court. At Frankfurter's suggestion, Brandeis offered Acheson a clerkship. Although Brandeis thought that some universal principles should be adhered to in legislating, he also thought that the law should reflect the "changing attitudes of society." A third mentor for Acheson was Oliver Wendell Holmes, also of the Supreme Court. Years later, after retiring from the State Department, Acheson called Holmes "the greatest man I have ever known"—a remarkable compliment considering the caliber of the leaders Acheson worked with in his career. With his style and charisma, Holmes commanded any room he entered. His political philosophy was similar to that of Frankfurter and Brandeis in that he believed "necessities of the time" should determine public policy.

Acheson continued nurturing an interest in politics after joining a Washington, D.C., law firm in 1921. He joined a political discussion group and the Maryland Democratic Party. Mostly, though, he focused on the law. He argued cases before the World Court at The Hague, Netherlands, and before the U.S. Supreme Court, winning about 20 percent of the latter, an impressive number that elevated his status in the Democratic Party.

Acheson campaigned hard for Democrat Al Smith in the 1928 presidential race. Smith lost, but the Democrat who ran in 1932—Franklin D. Roosevelt—won. When Roosevelt entered the White House the following March, Acheson was appointed undersecretary (second in command) of the treasury. After Acheson had been on the job for only six months, Roosevelt ordered him to try to devalue the dollar and induce inflation by buying gold at a higher price. (The value of the dollar was tied to the value of gold at the time.) Roosevelt hoped this would raise prices and, in turn, lift the United States out of the Great

inflation: a continuous rise in prices caused by an increase of available currency and credit beyond what the available goods and services can sustain

Franklin D. Roosevelt, the 32nd president of the United States, guided the nation through the Great Depression and World War II and was elected for an unprecedented four terms in office (1933-1945). Dean Acheson served in both the Treasury and State Departments during Roosevelt's presidency.

At the time Dean Acheson was moving up in the State Department, it was organized into several levels of secretaries. Ranking just below the secretary of state, the undersecretary of state served in place of the secretary of state if he was ever out of the office. Below the undersecretary of state were multiple assistant secretaries of state, each with a department to run, such as economic affairs or congressional relations. The State Department is currently organized in the same structure, although the undersecretary now holds the title of deputy secretary, and what were the assistant secretaries are now called under-secretaries of state.

Depression. Acheson refused, mainly on the grounds that the president did not have the legal authority to fix the price of gold. Roosevelt managed to push the plan through anyway. When news of some cabinet members' opposition to the plan leaked to the press, Roosevelt fired Acheson. Acheson later reconsidered his actions and became unsure whether he had done the right thing. He came to think that perhaps his duty to the president should have been more important than his objections to the plan.

Acheson remained out of government until December 1940, when Secretary of State Cordell Hull made him assistant secretary of state for economic affairs. World War II had been raging in Europe since September 1939. Already the Germans had captured much of the continent. In June 1941, they attacked eastward in a desperate attempt to crush the Soviet Union before winter. They failed. In 1942, they failed again. The Soviets turned the tide in 1943. In the Far East, Japan likewise fell short in its quest to dominate Asia and the Pacific Ocean. The United States rallied quickly from the surprise Japanese attack on Pearl Harbor in December 1941; by mid-1942, eventual U.S. victory in the Pacific was all but assured. As the nations struggled, Acheson focused less on waging the war and more on planning the peace. As it happened, no one did more to shape the postwar world than Dean Acheson.

In the Cabinet

In the four and a half years preceding his rise to leadership of the State Department in January 1949, Acheson compiled an extraordinary list of achievements. In fact, so often did he overshadow the men he worked for that it was as if Acheson were secretary of state.

Acheson's first major success occurred in July 1944, when he led the U.S. delegation to the Bretton Woods conference. Together with delegates from 43 other countries, Acheson helped to create the economic and financial systems that would govern the postwar order.

The International Monetary Fund (IMF) was designed to shore up national economies struggling with trade deficits caused by the war, while the International Bank for Reconstruction and Development (the World Bank) was established to make loans to member nations. The United States eventually contributed one-third of the start-up money for both, but Acheson had to fight to push the agreement through Congress in July 1945.

By then, Harry S. Truman had replaced Roosevelt, who had died in April. The new president, wrote Acheson, was "straightforward, decisive, simple, [and] entirely honest." Truman, equally impressed with Acheson, was thrilled when Secretary of State James Byrnes chose him as undersecretary of state in August. As second-in-command at the State Department for the next two years, Acheson took the lead in shaping U.S. anticommunist strategy.

The Bretton Woods conference at the Mount Washington Hotel in Bretton Woods, New Hampshire

trade deficit: an imbalance in a nation's trade in which imports are larger than exports

Vice President Harry S. Truman became president after Franklin Roosevelt's death in April 1945. Dean Acheson would have a strong influence on the new president's foreign policy.

Most U.S. leaders did not immediately realize the need to contain the Soviet Union, one of the U.S.'s wartime allies, as the war ended in summer 1945. Three events over the next year, however, convinced even diehard optimists that Soviet tyrant Josef Stalin was bent on dominating much of Europe and Asia.

The first event was Stalin's refusal to withdraw Soviet troops from Iran, which the Soviets had occupied with Great Britain in 1942 as a hedge against German invasion. Stalin had much to like in the Middle East—oil, of course, but also ice-free ports, almost as precious to an empire situated so far north. Although Stalin finally pulled out of Iran in May 1946, the crisis confirmed his desire to expand, especially into the oil-rich Middle East.

In the thick of the Iranian crisis in February, George F. Kennan, stationed in Moscow, telegraphed a lengthy explanation for Stalin's behavior. This was the second event. In short, Kennan argued that Stalin acted from a "traditional and instinctive Russian sense of insecurity." Throughout its history, Russia had suffered through numerous devastating invasions, the last being Germany's just years earlier. As a result, Russian leaders had "learned to seek security only in [a] patient but deadly struggle for [the] total destruction of [a] rival power. . . ." Stalin would never feel secure until every potential rival—the United States especially—ceased to exist. Fortunately, Kennan wrote, Stalin could be countered. He was "highly sensitive" to force and would withdraw if faced with "strong resistance" at a given point.

The third event also took place during the Iranian crisis. It was British wartime leader Winston Churchill's famous "iron curtain" speech, delivered in March 1946.

George F. Kennan (b. 1904), an American diplomat and expert on Russia, wrote a telegram that convinced many U.S. officials of the threat the Soviet Union posed.

Winston Churchill (1874-1965), served as prime minister of Britain twice, 1940-1945 and 1951-1955. He was out of office in 1946 when he sounded the "iron curtain" warning about Soviet expansion during his speech given in Fulton, Missouri.

"From Stettin in the Baltic [Sea] to Trieste in the Adriatic [Sea]," warned the famed statesman, "an iron curtain has descended across the continent [of Europe]." And Josef Stalin was to blame. Churchill's solution sounded much like Kennan's: "I am convinced that there is nothing [the Soviets] admire so much as strength, and there is nothing for which they have less respect than for military weakness." Churchill also made it clear that it was the United States, by virtue of its "primacy in power," that had to lead the resistance.

Truman and his aides were by now thoroughly anti-Soviet. Above all else, Stalin could not be allowed to overrun the capitalist democracies of Western Europe.

Economic aid to the area became the priority. But a current of isolationism still ran strong through Congress, where few members wanted to send billions of dollars to help the Europeans yet again. Acheson and the others knew they had to find some way to convince Congress to act before it was too late.

The opportunity came in February 1947, when Acheson learned that Great Britain could no longer afford to protect Greece from communist insurgents. It was Acheson's view that unless the U.S. stepped in and filled the breach, the Soviets would gain an important gateway (through Greece) to at least three continents: Europe, Asia, and Africa. To shock Congress into acting, Acheson chose to explain the threat in inflammatory terms (or, as he would later describe the tactic, to make it "clearer than truth").

insurgents: people who rebel by force against a particular authority, especially a government

In a meeting with congressional leaders, Truman, and Secretary of State George C. Marshall, Acheson compared the situation to "apples in a barrel infected by one rotten one." The "corruption" of Greece by the Soviets "would infect Iran and all to the east," while also spreading like a contagion southward to Africa and westward through Europe. Furthermore, he insisted, the United States could not isolate itself from the threat; if the rest of the world fell, the U.S. would wither on the vine. With Britain finished as a great power, "we and we alone" can block the "eager and ruthless opponent."

The legislators sat stunned after Acheson's impassioned warning. The fall of Greece was one thing, but here the president's advisors were talking about the collapse of the free world and even the United States. "Mr. President," suggested Arthur Vandenberg of the Senate Foreign Relations Committee, "if you will say that to the Congress and the country, I will support you and I believe that most of its members will do the same."

Truman agreed. Before a joint session of Congress in March, from text prepared mostly by Acheson, the president foresaw no less than disaster for the entire world

joint session: a special session of Congress in which the Senate and the House of Representatives meet in one place

The joint efforts of President Harry Truman and Dean Acheson steered U.S. foreign policy in a new direction. They are shown here with Australian prime minister Robert Menzies (right).

should Greece, and Turkey to its east, be allowed to collapse. Free peoples everywhere "look to us for support in maintaining their freedoms," he said. "If we falter in our leadership, we may endanger the peace of the world—and we shall surely endanger the welfare of this Nation." Finally, Truman made his point: "I believe that it must be the policy of the United States to support free peoples who are resisting attempted subjugation by armed minorities or by outside pressures."

This last statement, the Truman Doctrine, was staggering. The president's original goal was to gain economic and military aid (supplies but no troops) from Congress to ensure the freedom of Greece and Turkey. What he ended

up doing was declaring freedom for the whole world as his goal.

> Acheson and Truman [writes one historian] laid the groundwork for the belief, which would become ever more widely shared by government officials as well as the larger public, that the United States saw little alternative but to embark on the global containment of communism.

In other words, Acheson and Truman had no intention of mounting a worldwide effort at the time of Truman's speech; however, because they led Americans to believe that a global approach was necessary to ensure their nation's security, the public came to demand exactly that.

On the heels of Truman's speech, Acheson again employed his "clearer than truth" language in support of a European aid package he was helping to develop. In a May 1947 speech, he vividly described Europe's "utter exhaustion and economic dislocation." The U.S. would have to share its economic prosperity "if we are to preserve our own freedoms and our own democratic institutions." The speech was effective, and when Secretary Marshall revealed the economic relief package, the Marshall Plan, in June, Congress was leaning toward support.

Many lawmakers were still unsure, however. At this point, George Kennan wrote another blockbuster. In an article published in the July 1947 issue of *Foreign Affairs*, Kennan called for a "firm and vigilant containment of Russian expansive tendencies" by "the adroit and vigilant application of counterforce" wherever Stalin tried to expand. Kennan's words found many readers as lengthy excerpts were reprinted in *Life*, *Reader's Digest*, and newspapers nationwide.

The article only served to reinforce the message Acheson and Truman were proclaiming, that the U.S. had to assume global leadership in the fight against communism. (Indeed, Truman's anticommunist strategy, nameless so far, quickly became known as containment.) Thus, when a Stalin-ordered coup that gained the Communists control of the Eastern European nation of Czechoslovakia in February 1948 seemed to confirm all that Truman, Acheson, and Kennan had been saying, even the isolationists in Congress supported the Marshall Plan.

In October 1948, Great Britain, France, Belgium, the Netherlands, and Luxembourg invited the United States to join the Brussels Defense Pact, a military defense alliance. Acheson quickly took the lead in securing Senate approval. Considering that the United States had never been part of a peacetime military alliance, he could have expected a tough sell. Stalin's continued provocations eased his task. The Soviet tyrant's latest move was to blockade the

This cartoon shows Josef Stalin trying to prevent a ball labeled "Marshall Plan" from hitting the basket of European recovery. The success of the Marshall Plan, which provided economic aid to countries devastated by World War II, would have interfered with the Soviet dictator's efforts to gain power in Europe.

German city of Berlin in June 1948. The Berlin Blockade was the last straw for the U.S. Senate. In July 1949, it ratified U.S. membership in the European alliance, renamed the North Atlantic Treaty Organization (NATO).

Even as NATO became operational in Europe, communists were overrunning China. But these communists weren't Soviet puppets. Acheson, who had become secretary of state in January 1949, saw no reason to try to stop them. He intended to let the Chinese Communists gain control, then do what he could to keep them independent of Stalin's rule—and perhaps even keep them friendly to the U.S. The secretary was attacked by anticommunist members of Congress after the Communists gained control of China in October 1949. Until the end of his term in

On August 24, 1949, President Harry Truman signed the document that implemented the North Atlantic Treaty Organization.

Mao Zedong (1893-1976) led the Communists that took over China in 1949. He was chief of state of the People's Republic of China from 1949 to 1959 and chairman of China's Communist Party from 1931 until his death.

1953, Acheson was dogged mercilessly for having "lost" China.

Communists were also active in Korea. When the Americans and Soviets liberated the Korean peninsula from the Japanese at the end of World War II, they temporarily divided the finger of land into north (communist) and south (noncommunist, but under an authoritarian regime). Acheson never considered South Korean independence vital to American security, and he purposely excluded the nation from the U.S.'s "defense perimeter." In June 1950, North Korea took advantage of the United States's apparent lack of interest and invaded South Korea.

Truman had little choice in his response. His and Acheson's language in the Truman Doctrine had declared

America's intention to stand for freedom everywhere. To back away from the commitment now could harm the nation's credibility, not only among the weakened allies in Europe, but also in Africa, the Middle East, and elsewhere in Asia. With United Nations approval, Truman ordered American soldiers into Korea. Containment had now become global in deed as well as in word.

Looking Forward

More than a century earlier, in 1823, Greece had been struggling for independence from the Ottoman Empire. In an early draft of the Monroe Doctrine, mostly written by Secretary of State John Quincy Adams, President James Monroe included supportive words to the Greeks. Adams immediately objected. The policy's main goal, he argued,

The Ottoman Empire was a very powerful state that dominated southeastern Europe and the Middle East for more than 600 years. Founded by Turkish tribes in the late 1200s, the empire was defeated in World War I and broken up in 1918. The modern state of Turkey arose out of its collapse.

Dean Acheson being sworn in as secretary of state on January 21, 1949

was to keep the Europeans from intervening in the New World. How could the United States expect Europe to stay out of "its" hemisphere if the U.S. went abroad "in search of monsters to destroy?" Monroe dropped the reference, and his doctrine remained an endorsement of complete American isolation from the "sordid" affairs of the Old World.

The Truman Doctrine, on the other hand, argued that U.S. interests had expanded beyond the Western Hemisphere. It still warned against colonization and intervention, only this time the target was the Soviet Union, instead of the Russian-controlled Holy Alliance of Adams's day. The U.S. would still protect its interests, but, according to Truman and Acheson, those interests had grown to include the freedom of other nations—even nations within Europe. Instead of being concerned only with the New World, the U.S. was now willing to become involved in the affairs of the entire world.

Truman and Acheson had left office by the end of the Korean War in July 1953. While technically a draw, the outcome proved containment worked; the communists had been turned back, the prewar border between North and South Korea reestablished. But the "victory" cost the lives of more than 54,000 U.S. soldiers and wounded another 105,000; shattered relations with China and North Korea; and tripled American defense spending. An even more costly effect was the anticommunist hysteria that gripped the nation after 1950. The public now demanded worldwide containment.

After leaving office in January 1953, Acheson continued to address foreign policy issues in books, articles, and lectures. During the 1960s, he advised Presidents John F. Kennedy and Lyndon B. Johnson. As part of Kennedy's "Executive Committee" during the Cuban Missile Crisis in October 1962, Acheson favored American air strikes against the nuclear missile sites that the Soviets were building on the island just 90 miles off the coast of Florida.

Unknown to him or the other Americans, the Soviets had already installed 98 nuclear missiles on the island. Had Kennedy taken Acheson's advice and bombed the island, the result likely would have been nuclear war.

Acheson was equally adamant in advising President Johnson to respond forcefully to communist aggression in Vietnam. That was in early July 1965. Within the month, Johnson committed American combat troops to the region, where they became mired in a war they could not win. Again, Acheson's aggressiveness proved counterproductive.

Dean Acheson died on October 12, 1971. During his long career in the State Department, he did more than any other person, except perhaps Josef Stalin, to prod the United States out of its isolationist past. U.S. intervention probably stopped Stalin from overrunning Europe. Containment certainly saved the Middle East and Korea. Acheson's method of making things "clearer than truth" also extended U.S. commitments far beyond what he intended, past points vital to its survival and prosperity, and beyond what the country could actually handle.

An American soldier passes a destroyed North Korean tank. More than 54,000 Americans lost their lives in the Korean War; North and South Korean losses were at least 10 times that number. The conflict ended in 1953 with the reestablishment of the prewar border between North and South Korea.

★ ★ 6 ★ ★

JOHN FOSTER DULLES

Massive Retaliation

For John Foster Dulles, braving the elements in the rugged outdoors was the truest test of human endurance. Sailing in rough weather aboard his boat—with ice-cold waves crashing over the vessel's deck, drenching him and his crew for hours on end—especially captivated Dulles. His drive to overcome adversity went beyond merely surviving the harsh and unpredictable weather. Dulles demanded total victory, with honor and on his terms. None of his crew, for instance, ate until they had gone for a swim. And sleep? Dulles would sail all night, not allowing himself a wink. When port was reached and victory secured, he would relax, satisfied he had fought the good fight.

From Dulles's point of view, the American ship of state, tossing amid the treacherous waters of the Cold War, was not all that different from his twin-masted sailboat. To achieve victory with honor, presidents had to be willing to push their countries to the very brink of destruction. Those leaders unwilling to do so risked foundering on the shoals of total and humiliating defeat.

The Formative Years ────────────

Born in Washington, D.C., on February 25, 1888, "Foster" was the son of Allen Macy Dulles, a minister, and Edith Foster Dulles, daughter of John W. Foster (secretary of state from 1892 to 1893). Edith's brother-in-law was

As secretary of state, John Foster Dulles (1888-1959) used the skills he learned in sailing to guide the U.S. through the rough waters of the Cold War. He believed that the threat of massive nuclear retaliation was necessary to defend the nation from its enemies.

John Watson Foster (1836-1917), John Foster Dulles's grandfather on his mother's side and secretary of state from 1892 to 1893

Robert Lansing, an up-and-coming international lawyer who would serve as secretary of state from 1915 to 1920.

It was his grandfather Foster who taught John Foster and his younger brother Allen to sail and fish on Lake Ontario, near the Dulles family home in eastern New York. On summer vacations, when the day's catch was cooking, he and Robert Lansing—Uncle "Bert"—often transfixed the boys with tales of international diplomacy. To Allen and Edith Dulles fell the responsibility of shaping the spiritual lives of their sons and three daughters. Young Foster grew into a disciplined and diligent student who graduated from high school at 15.

Following a year in France and a year with Grandfather Foster in Washington, Dulles entered New Jersey's Princeton University in the autumn of 1904. During his junior year, he joined his grandfather at an international peace conference in Europe. It proved a captivating introduction to diplomacy. When Dulles returned to Europe after graduation in 1908, he took a few courses in international law at the University of Paris. From that point he was hooked. In 1909, he entered George Washington Law School in Washington, D.C., and blew through the three-year course in just two. By the end of 1911, Dulles was practicing international law in New York City.

When the U.S. entered World War I in 1917, Dulles joined the army as a lawyer. He wound up participating in the Paris peace conference in 1919 as legal advisor to one of the American representatives. (Fighting had ended the previous November.) President Woodrow Wilson's failure to convince the U.S. Senate to ratify the resulting Treaty of Paris (more commonly known as the Treaty of Versailles) taught Dulles a lifelong lesson—in democracies, foreign policies must always reflect the public will. Wilson had unwisely ignored the advice of opposition senators while negotiating the Versailles treaty, which included the charter for the worldwide League of Nations. The senators responded by rejecting the treaty and American

The opening session of the League of Nations on November 15, 1920, in Geneva, Switzerland

membership in the League. While to some degree their move was simply based on a personal dislike of Wilson, the greatest factor in their defeat of the Versailles treaty was the public's desire to return to prewar isolation.

Dulles left the army in 1919 and spent the next two decades practicing international business law. Along the way, he dabbled in diplomacy, mostly as a consultant to the U.S. Treasury regarding German war reparations and repayment of the U.S.'s wartime loans to allies France and Great Britain. (Dulles wanted to reduce the loans to bolster European economies.) He represented the United States at the Berlin Conference in 1933, called to tackle Germany's worsening debt situation. After 1938, Dulles addressed these and other foreign policy issues through various writings and speeches.

As militarism gripped Europe and Asia in the 1920s and 1930s, Dulles placed much of the blame on the Versailles pact, which he thought was especially hard on Germany. Against President Wilson's protests, the Allies, especially France and Great Britain, had forced the Germans to accept steep reparations; massive disarmament; the loss of land, population, and colonies; and a "war guilt clause," which placed all responsibility for the war on Germany and its allies. Although the treaty was never properly enforced, the Germans stewed in humiliation—they thought any punishment was unjust. Their rage and feeling of utter helplessness (as well as the fact that their military was never reduced as outlined in the treaty) eventually helped lift the vengeful Adolf Hitler to national power in 1933.

Dulles thought another destabilizing factor was the European Allies' interpretation of the treaty. For instance, Dulles thought the Allies should have focused on an article in the League charter that allowed for reconsideration of treaties that no longer promoted peace. The Allies focused instead on two articles meant to prevent armed aggression. Dulles argued that their goal was to prevent all change to the existing international structure, both peaceful and violent.

Adolf Hitler (1889-1945) led the Nazi movement in Germany in the 1930s and 1940s. During World War II, the fascist Nazis took large portions of Europe by force and exterminated millions of people, including six million Jews.

Dulles believed that disagreements and change were inevitable among people: "There will always be differences of opinion . . . and always ways will be found of settling them." Either nations would work together to find peaceful ways of settling disputes among themselves and within their borders, or wars would continue.

Although Dulles supposed that tyrants like Hitler would always exist "to lead the masses in ways of violence," he mostly blamed the international system for Hitler's rise. A new way had to be found to prevent "the many from feeling that they are subject to power which is exercised without regard for their welfare and which condemns them to inequalities and indignities." If this were done, thugs like Hitler would never gain power in the first place. How to empower the peoples of the world to achieve freedom and self-fulfillment peacefully became Dulles's driving obsession.

In 1937, Dulles met Thomas Dewey, a successful U.S. prosecutor. Dulles, by then president of his law firm, offered the younger man a senior partnership. Dewey ran for district attorney of New York County instead. He won, and his star continued rising in the Republican Party. Dewey was elected to three terms as governor of New York. He just missed the Republican presidential nomination in 1940, then gained the nod in 1944 and 1948. Both tries failed, but the latter attempt against President Harry Truman just barely did. In all three contests, Dewey relied on Dulles, seasoned international lawyer and occasional diplomat, for foreign policy advice.

As Dewey's foreign affairs expert—and likely secretary of state if Dewey won the White House—Dulles became a leading Republican voice on international relations. He used his standing during World War II (1939-1945) to drum up public support for U.S. participation in a postwar successor organization to the League of Nations. Indeed, despite the fact that the Republicans boasted some of the country's best known isolationists, Dulles's concept of global cooperation went even further than what Democratic President Franklin Roosevelt was proposing by 1943.

Thomas Dewey (1902-1971) campaigning for president. Although predicted to win, Dewey lost the 1948 election to Harry Truman in one of the greatest political upsets in American history.

Roosevelt had in mind an organization controlled by four "policemen"—the wartime Allies of the United States, the Soviet Union, China, and Great Britain. France, another Allied nation, was later included. Dulles feared the proposed organization would end up a tool of the victors to maintain a postwar status quo, the way he thought the League of Nations had.

Dulles wanted more—a federal union modeled on the system of the U.S., in which nations subordinated themselves to a government of the whole, like the relationship of the American states to the national government in Washington, D.C. Dulles had come to view nationalism as "the most powerful and dangerous force in the world." Leaders, even of democracies, easily manipulated their populations by using "other-nation-devil" and "own-nation-hero" arguments. Peoples whipped into "a sense of moral superiority" were not prone to the give-and-take needed to solve problems peacefully. Dulles argued that if people identified less with their own nations and more with an international community, they would be less likely to make war on one another.

nationalism: devotion to one's nation to the extent that the nation is more important than the individual. Nationalism may also refer to this type of devotion to groupings other than nations, such as race, ethnicity, or culture.

Dulles's concept was not what the people got, however (nor what they would accept). The United Nations, with the five policemen making up the five permanent members of the ruling Security Council (the "perm five"), officially came into being in the spring of 1945. Dulles was not confident that the UN would be an effective agent of peaceful change. It did little to eliminate the "nation" as the supreme political authority. In fact, with the perm five able to veto any UN action, it seemed the perfect tool for the most powerful to maintain their status. Still, like most Americans, Dulles hoped the victorious Allies who made up the perm five might continue to cooperate to solve the world's problems.

By the summer of 1946, Dulles realized that confrontation, not cooperation, would most likely characterize the postwar period. The problem was the Soviet Union. It

John Foster Dulles (far left) with Eleanor Roosevelt, UN delegate and former first lady, and Adlai Stevenson, a prominent Democrat of the time, at a meeting of the United Nations in 1946. All three wear headphones to hear translations of speeches made by non-English-speaking delegates.

had made threatening moves toward the oil-rich Middle East and continued to occupy and oppress Eastern Europe. Even before the U.S. entrance into the war in 1941, Dulles had considered how "a highly armed Russia facing a disarmed and socially chaotic Europe would be a grave menace." He had hoped a powerful UN might neutralize the Soviets. That now seemed unlikely, given the Soviets' perm five veto.

Over the next few years, in speeches, magazine articles, and even a book, Dulles discussed the threat. The Soviets' main foreign policy goal, he concluded, was to ensure their nation's security by surrounding themselves with allies. Since they already occupied a buffer of satellite states in Eastern Europe, they were unlikely to invade farther for fear of drawing an American atomic response. To win additional allies, the Soviets instead would foment rebellion among oppressed peoples. This they would do through economic and military aid and by manipulating the downtrodden emotionally with "other-nation-devil"-type propaganda. The Soviets thought that once the rebellions had taken place, the new governments would accept Moscow's lead.

Dulles admonished American leaders not to use "other-nation-devil" rhetoric themselves. Rather than attack the Soviets, U.S. leaders should instead put their own country in order by eradicating inequalities and ensuring freedom and justice at home. Then the United States could be a true "power of attraction" to the rest of the world. What Dulles did not want was simple military containment of Soviet expansion. The expense would be too great, for one thing. Besides, in a world divided "between those who would maintain the status quo [the U.S. in this case] and those who would change the status quo . . . [t]hose who would sustain the status quo inevitably are defeated." Americans must not defend their institutions just as they are, Dulles insisted, but "seek even more ardently to make them better than they now are."

At the same time he was expressing these beliefs, Dulles became more involved in politics. He advised Dewey in the 1948 presidential race and ran himself (unsuccessfully) for the U.S. Senate in 1950. During these years, the bipartisan tone that had characterized much of wartime policymaking disappeared. By 1952, the Republicans were desperate to win back the presidency. Dulles's speeches and writings became sharp, partisan pronouncements. Although he had publicly supported much of the Democrats' containment strategy, he now sowed public doubt about parts of the policy.

Dulles the partisan spoke more of a Soviet "menace," whereas earlier he had used more tempered characterizations like "challenge" or "competition." In an early 1952

partisan: a devoted and fervent supporter of a party or cause, often used in regard to political parties

Life magazine article, "A Policy of Boldness," Dulles wrote of a moral law that "has been trampled by the Soviet rulers," a violation for which "they can and should be made to pay." He whipped up fear: "We are marked down for destruction [he said in October] by those who today control one-third of the world." Earlier talk of coexisting peacefully with communism until its death by neglect was replaced with an urgent appeal to end the "peril" before the "gigantic expenditures" of containment led to "strength nowhere and bankruptcy everywhere."

Why did Dulles change? His inflammatory language was meant to appeal mostly to followers of Senator Joseph McCarthy of Wisconsin, the feared anticommunist crusader. "McCarthyism" was at its peak during the early

During the early 1950s, Senator Joseph McCarthy (1908-1957) conducted a series of investigations of Americans—including top government officials—accused of being Communists.

Robert Taft (1889-1953) was a Republican leader in the U.S. Senate from 1939 to 1953. A conservative, Taft lost the 1948 Republican presidential nomination to Thomas Dewey in part due to his isolationist views, which were no longer popular.

1950s, and anyone who wanted to make it in politics had to denounce communism. Dulles also had to help unite the isolationist and internationalist wings of the Republican Party. Dwight Eisenhower, the Republican nominee, was an internationalist, but he wasn't the most powerful man in the party. Senator Robert Taft, an isolationist from Ohio, was. Taft supported McCarthy. He also hated the steep defense budgets of the current Truman administration. If Dulles, who hoped to serve as Eisenhower's secretary of state, ever wanted to win Senate approval for his foreign policies, he had to appease Taft.

Keeping all this in mind, Dulles proposed a new containment strategy. The Western democracies, he wrote, had to "develop the will and organize the means to retaliate instantly against open aggression by Red armies, so that, if it occurred anywhere, we could and would strike back where it hurts, by means of our choosing." In other words, the Communists would be warned explicitly that a Russian or Chinese invasion anywhere could draw an American atomic response against Moscow or Beijing. (Dulles called

During the Cold War, posters like this one, which depicts a man protecting the Philippines from the encroaching hammer and sickle symbol of the Soviet Union, encouraged Americans to oppose communism.

the atomic arsenal a "community punishing force" even though the bombs would be American. He never said as much, but Dulles expected the United States to assume much of the policeman's role he earlier had envisioned for the United Nations.)

Dulles's strategy differed from Truman's, which met aggression where it happened and with a similar level of counterforce. The problem with Truman's strategy was that it required a huge military stationed at all potential hot spots. Dulles's strategy did not. A few big bombs were cheaper than big armies, and an unequivocal warning would prevent any miscalculation on the part of the Communists. (Dulles believed the Soviet Union ordered or at least allowed communist North Korea to invade non-communist South Korea in 1950 because the U.S. had not warned against the move.)

There was a downside to Dulles's strategy. Dulles could not advocate striking hard against the Soviets and still maintain his stance against nations using "other-nation-devil" propaganda. He now had to denounce communism forcefully and give up on his dream of international cooperation. In short, Dulles would have to do all the things he had always preached against.

In the Cabinet

Following Dwight Eisenhower's victory in November 1952, the new president picked Dulles to head the Department of State. As a Republican, Eisenhower hoped to reduce defense expenditures and taxes. As an internationalist, he advocated a global leadership role for the United States. Dulles's policy of nuclear deterrence fit nearly perfectly.

Immediately upon assuming office, Dulles sailed for rougher waters. In a televised address in January 1953, he warned of "enemies who are plotting our destruction"—the "800 million people" then living under communism who

President-elect Dwight D. Eisenhower (1890-1969) chose John Foster Dulles as secretary of state in part because none of the other candidates would have satisfied the powerful Republican senator Robert Taft.

Dulles (far side of table, third from left) reports to President Eisenhower (immediate right of Dulles) and other members of the cabinet.

were "being forged into a vast weapon of fighting power backed by industrial production and modern weapons that include atomic bombs." When Soviet tyrant Josef Stalin died two months later and the Soviet leaders signaled their desire to adopt a policy of "peaceful coexistence and competition," Dulles dismissed the initiative out of hand. It was a trick, he told Eisenhower, and backed his suspicion by quoting passages from Stalin's communist writings. Just a few years earlier, Dulles had believed that national interests, not communist ideology, drove the Soviets. Now he claimed the opposite. If the new Dulles was right, then no communists could be trusted.

In early September 1954, Communist China opened fire on the small islands of Quemoy and Matsu two miles off its east coast. The islands were held by Chinese Nationalists who had fled the country in 1949 following their defeat by the Communists in the Chinese civil war. The Nationalists had taken refuge on Taiwan, an island about 100 miles off the mainland, and had claimed Quemoy and Matsu as part of their frontier. Chiang Kai-shek, the Nationalist leader, was threatening "holy war" to regain China and was negotiating a defense alliance with the United States. Considering the Nationalists out-laws with no rights to any of the land they occupied, the Chinese Communists bombarded Quemoy and Matsu in preparation for invading Taiwan.

Dulles believed the United States had few options. For one thing, the U.S. had long considered itself China's pro-tector, at least since the days of Secretary of State John Hay. That's one reason the Truman administration had

Chiang Kai-shek (1887-1975) led the Nationalist Republic in China for almost 20 years before his party lost power to the Communists.

A Chinese Nationalist soldier keeps watch outside the Nationalist army's bunker on Quemoy. The bunker's entrance bears the following words in Chinese: "If you want to live a happy life, you must be an anticommunist."

faced the wrath of Congress for "losing" the mainland to the Communists in 1949. Dulles was not about to lose Taiwan and face a similar congressional backlash. The problem was, Americans had never considered Quemoy or Matsu worth defending. The islands weren't the least bit vital to Taiwan's security—the U.S. Navy could easily scuttle an attacking force—and they certainly didn't mean life or death for the United States. Even Eisenhower had originally believed that "Quemoy is not our ship." Dulles disagreed. As he saw it, every time communists anywhere were "permitted to gobble up" part of the world, they added to Moscow's power. Sooner or later, "the Soviet world will be so powerful that no corner of the world will be safe."

Back on the islands, Communist planes joined the artillery barrage from the mainland. Chiang responded with air strikes against Communist ports and shipping. Tensions escalated further in January 1955 when Communist troops maneuvered for an apparent invasion of the islands. In response, the U.S. Congress turned up the heat. Lawmakers passed a resolution authorizing Eisenhower to use any force necessary, including atomic bombs, to defend the islands. (Some observers, however, including Winston Churchill—Britain's indomitable wartime leader and avowed hater of communism—thought it absurd to risk World War III over the islands.)

Dulles now had the "means" and the "will" required of his deterrent strategy. He warned the Communists that any invasion of Quemoy and Matsu could bring a nuclear response from the United States. Meanwhile, Dulles downplayed the destructiveness of nuclear weapons to ensure that the American public backed the threat. In reality, the "weapons of precision" Dulles insisted could "utterly destroy military targets without endangering unrelated civilian centers" did not exist. Statistics showed that from 12 to 14 million people stood to lose their lives if military targets on the Chinese mainland opposite Quemoy were attacked with even the smallest atomic bombs. The situation was grave: "[B]efore this problem is solved," Dulles told the president, "I believe there is at least an even chance that the United States will have to go to war."

Near the end of April 1955, in part because of pressure from other Asian nations and from Africa, the Chinese Communists backed away from their threat to invade and declared their wish to avoid war with the United States. The storm subsided. Because the Soviet Union had offered no support to China, it appeared to Dulles and Eisenhower that the Soviets had flinched, just as the Chinese had. Better yet, ties between Moscow and Beijing were weakening. Dulles's strategy had succeeded. The administration, Eisenhower later wrote, had successfully sailed

artillery: large-caliber weapons, such as cannons or missile launchers; also the branch of the army that specializes in using these weapons

"through treacherous cross-currents with one channel leading to peace with honor and a hundred channels leading to war or dishonor."

But the crisis was not over. Over the next three and a half years, Chiang moved 100,000 soldiers to Quemoy and its surrounding islands. Again provoked, the Communists resumed bombing in August 1958. When an invasion seemed imminent, Dulles reissued the threat of nuclear retaliation. This time, however, he struck a tidal wave of negative world opinion. Great Britain, America's steadfast ally, voiced support for China's claim to Quemoy. Even combative former secretary of state Dean Acheson insisted the island was not worth "a single American life."

Driving the public's backlash was their realization of the Soviet Union's growing nuclear capability. *Sputnik*, the first artificial satellite, had been launched by the Soviets in October 1957, proving that they could send a nuclear warhead anywhere in the world within 30 minutes. By the time of the second Quemoy crisis, the Soviets had some 30 nuclear-tipped ballistic missiles in their arsenal. And they didn't hesitate to play the new hand, either. In September, they warned the United States that any nuclear attack on China would open the United States to similar destruction.

Faced with eroding public support and, for the first time, a real counterthreat, Eisenhower ordered Dulles to back away from the brink. In a press conference in late September, the secretary chided Chiang for being "rather foolish" to station his troops on Quemoy in the first place. The wise move, he suggested, would be for the Nationalist leader to send part of his force back to Taiwan. Dulles then suggested a ceasefire. Dependent as he was on the Americans, Chiang had no choice but to agree. The Communists followed suit in order to create the appearance that they were coming out ahead. Still, Dulles had never officially rescinded his threat of nuclear retaliation.

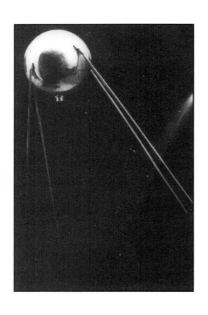

Although only 184 pounds and 23 inches in diameter, Sputnik 1 *was visible in the night sky and transmitted a beeping signal for 21 days before it reentered the atmosphere and burned up.*

Looking Forward

Eight months later, on May 24, 1959, John Foster Dulles died of cancer. From that point on, Eisenhower focused less on confronting the Soviets and more on opening a constructive dialogue with them. Dulles's strategy of nuclear deterrence had been justifiable before the Soviets had developed the ability to destroy the United States. Even after that point, Dulles had still been willing to step to the brink and risk everything. Eisenhower, always less confrontational than his secretary of state, was not.

What didn't change was American distrust and fear of all things communist. Dulles's insistence that any gain for communism was a potentially devastating loss for the free world remained. No distinction was made between Soviet client states and nations that, while communist in nature, were fiercely opposed to Moscow's control. All were communist, and therefore, all were considered dangerous to U.S. security.

The Dulles Airport, named to honor John Foster Dulles, was designed by Eero Saarinen and completed in 1962. It is located in Chantilly, Virginia, and serves the Washington, D.C., area.

$\star$ $\star$ *7* $\star$ $\star$

HENRY ALFRED KISSINGER

Détente and the Balance of Power

At the end of the 1960s, the United States and the Soviet Union no longer had control of the world. Other nations were rapidly gaining ground, militarily and economically. By 1964, Great Britain, France, and China had all developed their own nuclear weapons. Japan was gaining more and more economic influence.

With less power to control world events, leaders in Washington were naturally apprehensive. The appearance of another communist giant with atomic weapons—China—was especially unsettling. Two Americans, however, did not fear the new development. In fact, they saw the whole thing as a tremendous stroke of good fortune. In 1968, president-elect Richard Nixon was one. The other was his soon-to-be foreign policy chief, Henry Kissinger.

The Formative Years

Heinz Alfred Kissinger, first child of Paula and Louis Kissinger, was born in Fürth, Germany, on May 27, 1923. Less than six months later, Adolf Hitler attempted to overthrow Germany's government. Although it failed, his coup attempt was an ominous sign for the Jewish Kissingers. In Hitler's mind, Jews were the cowards behind Germany's

Henry Kissinger (b. 1923) at a press conference in October 1974. Kissinger orchestrated a three-power balance during the Cold War, enlisting the Chinese on the side of the United States in order to subdue the Soviets with a larger military threat.

surrender to the Allies at the end of World War I in November 1918. Even worse, Hitler was sure the Jews had engineered the Communist Revolution in Russia in 1917 and now intended a similar takeover of Germany. By the time of Heinz's birth, Hitler's anti-Semitic tirades were finding listeners across the country.

As Heinz grew up, he faced a steady stream of abuse: segregation, racial slurs, even beatings from the brain-washed Hitler Youth. As a Jewish friend of Kissinger's recalled years later, the persecution was so prevalent it "was like the air we breathed." Louis Kissinger was forced to quit teaching school when the Nazis declared Jews unworthy to instruct Germans. By August 1938, he and Paula had had enough. They took Heinz and his younger brother, Walter, and immigrated to the United States. The experience was not lost on Heinz. People like Hitler never bowed to reason or high ideals, the young man realized, only to superior force.

Anti-Semitic propaganda displayed in a shoe store window in Germany in 1933

Heinz embraced his new culture when the Kissingers arrived in New York City. He changed his name to Henry and did his best to fit in at George Washington High School. After graduating in 1940, he worked days and took night classes at the City College of New York. Despite a voracious appetite for learning, Henry never made it through City College; he was drafted into the U.S. Army in February 1943. Nineteen months later, he was back in Germany, this time as part of the Allied offensive that would crush the Nazis.

Thanks to Fritz Kraemer, Kissinger was not on the frontline of the fighting. Kraemer, another German exile, worked for division headquarters, briefing soldiers on what to expect when they entered Germany. He and Kissinger became fast friends after meeting at one of the briefings. Before Kissinger knew it, Kraemer had him pulled from the infantry and driving a headquarters jeep.

A few months later, Kraemer began overseeing the occupation of towns within the division's sector. He picked Kissinger to root out suspected Nazis. Kissinger succeeded brilliantly. By blocking out any hate or contempt for his former tormentors, he was able to cultivate relationships with captured Nazis, then use them to bring in others still at large.

Kissinger left Germany in July 1947. From Kraemer he had developed a passion for history, and he now followed his friend's advice to complete his college education at a first-class university. Kissinger chose Harvard. Secretary of State George C. Marshall, the top U.S. general during the war, had recently announced his "plan" at Harvard's graduation ceremony. The Marshall Plan, as it would be known, was Marshall's blueprint for jump-starting the economies of Europe. When 24-year-old Henry Kissinger arrived, Harvard was abuzz with enthusiasm for the country's new activism.

Kissinger breezed through his undergraduate years with just one *B* to mar an otherwise perfect academic

George Catlett Marshall (1880-1959) won the Nobel Peace Prize in 1953 for his efforts to reconstruct Europe after World War II.

Klemens von Metternich (1773-1859) was the Austrian minister of foreign affairs from 1809 to 1848 and helped form the alliance that defeated Napoleon. He also contributed to establishing the balance of power that endured after Napoleon's fall.

transcript. It was enough to ensure he graduated among the top one percent of his class in 1950. Next came graduate school, where Kissinger researched and wrote a book-length dissertation. His topic was a duo of nineteenth-century European diplomats famous for creating a continent-wide "balance of power" in the wake of French emperor Napoleon Bonaparte's downfall in 1815. The balance, as Kissinger noted, ushered in a period of relative peace for Europe that lasted almost 100 years. The two statesmen—Klemens von Metternich, foreign minister of Austria, and Lord Castlereagh (Robert Stewart), foreign secretary of Great Britain—worked with their counterparts from Prussia, Russia, and France to achieve peace by trading territory until a rough equality existed among their states. The result was that no one was dominant. Had one of the powers tried to force an issue, the others would have joined together to stop it. Stability reigned and, with it, peace and prosperity.

As Kissinger surveyed the global landscape over the next two decades, he came to believe a similar balance was emerging. For many years after World War II, the United States and the Soviet Union recognized just two centers of world power—themselves. They struggled against each other, believing gains for one to be devastating losses for the other. The advantage swung back and forth between the two superpowers, easily upsetting global stability and making peace very difficult to maintain. Over time, however, other centers of power appeared. Western Europe and Japan emerged as economic powers in the 1950s and 1960s, while Western Europe and China developed notable military strength. China, furthermore, grew into a major ideological power, challenging the Soviet Union for sponsorship of communist movements throughout the world. A world with multiple centers of power, Kissinger believed, was structurally more stable than a world with just two. And it would be less taxing on the superpowers, too, because the burden of maintaining stability would be shared with others.

The real challenge for the Americans would be to manipulate the balance to their advantage. While Kissinger increased his influence throughout the years—as author of foreign policy books and articles; Harvard professor of international relations from 1957 to 1968; and foreign policy advisor to Nelson Rockefeller, unsuccessful challenger for the Republican presidential nomination in 1968—he refined a strategy to do just that. When Richard Nixon won the White House in November 1968, Kissinger hoped to serve in some capacity in the new president's State Department. On November 26, Nixon appointed him national security advisor instead. It was a position that ultimately gave Kissinger more diplomatic responsibilities and power than the secretary of state, and, at times, even more than the president.

In the Cabinet

Historically, the secretary of state had been the president's chief foreign policy advisor and the nation's top diplomat. This wasn't so in Nixon's administration. Nixon didn't trust the State Department. He considered it a sluggish bureaucracy that couldn't react fast enough in the changing modern world. He skirted the problem by avoiding the department as much as possible and letting Kissinger handle the important diplomacy. As a result, Kissinger was the *de facto*—meaning actually, rather than officially—U.S. secretary of state.

The overriding diplomatic goal for Richard Nixon and Henry Kissinger as they entered office in January 1969 was to negotiate an end to the war in Vietnam. Since 1965, some 30,000 Americans had died fighting the communist insurgency in South Vietnam. As a candidate, Nixon had

American soldiers in Vietnam carrying a wounded comrade. In an effort to contain communism, the U.S. had backed the leaders of South Vietnam, providing military advisors and aid starting in 1956. By the end of 1969, more than 500,000 U.S. soldiers were in Vietnam—with the war's end nowhere in sight.

In 1954, Ho Chi Minh (1890-1969), leader of Vietnam's Communist movement, defeated the French, who had occupied Vietnam for almost 200 years. Although Ho accepted arms and supplies from the Soviet Union and China, he was only using the two powers to achieve independence for his country. The North Vietnamese continued to rely on Soviet and Chinese aid after Ho's death.

promised to pull U.S. forces out by the end of his first term, but he was unwilling to risk the reputation of the United States by just quitting the war. He wanted concessions by the North Vietnamese first. The trouble was, the Communists were winning the war and had little incentive to concede anything. They had a weak spot, however: their sizeable reliance on Soviet and Chinese weapons, food, and fuel. Nixon and Kissinger knew that to end the war, they would have to convince the Communist giants to withhold support from their Vietnamese ally.

The key was to reestablish a balance of power. In Southeast Asia, Soviet and Chinese power was arrayed against that of the United States. It was two against one and the two were winning. Nixon and Kissinger's goal was to become one of the two. They would try to improve relations with both Communist powers—a policy that came to be known as détente, French for "relaxation" or "easing"—then join forces with one to moderate the behavior of the other. This could work in Vietnam to force one or both to withdraw support from the North Vietnamese, but it might also work to curb Soviet- or Chinese-sponsored aggression elsewhere. Furthermore, a triangular balance of power could help with other issues, like motivating the Soviets to accept limits on the production of nuclear weapons.

Nixon and Kissinger approached China first. The Soviets feared the Chinese because they were competing with them for the allegiance of peoples throughout the developing world who were fighting wars of national liberation. (The war in Southeast Asia was a good example, with the Vietnamese Communists fighting to eliminate foreign control of Vietnam. The Russians and Chinese hoped that by aiding independence movements, they would gain allies in the resulting nations.) Any improvement in relations between the United States and China would certainly alarm leaders in Moscow, who might then curb support for North Vietnam so as not to antagonize the Americans further.

Building a diplomatic link with China proved difficult, however. As Nixon and Kissinger had feared, the process bogged down in the procedural maze of the State Department. Nixon lost little time in circumventing the department altogether and asking the president of Pakistan in 1969 to approach China with Nixon's request to begin new diplomatic relations. Nixon repeated his request when the Pakistani president visited Washington, D.C., in October 1970. Afraid of the Soviets, the Chinese were eager to meet with a representative of the president. Kissinger made the historic trip in July 1971.

While the North Vietnamese took note of the burgeoning relationship between the Americans and Chinese, they hardly moderated their behavior. Even Nixon's visit

to China in February 1972 did nothing to halt the Communists, who launched a devastating military offensive against South Vietnam the following month. The Chinese did press the North Vietnamese to end the war, but they were unwilling to go as far as terminating support. Kissinger next warned the Soviets that Nixon's planned trip to Moscow in May could be called off if they didn't rein in the North Vietnamese. Again, there was little noticeable effect. Either the Soviets made little effort to halt North Vietnam or, more likely, the North Vietnamese simply ignored them. Kissinger's triangular balance of power didn't seem to be working.

Henry Kissinger, pursuing détente with China, meets with Mao Zedong, the leader of China's Communist Party from 1931 to 1976.

Richard Nixon (1913-1994) prepared carefully for his historic trip to China. He had Kissinger meet twice with the Chinese beforehand to ensure that there would be no diplomatic problems during the official visit. Nixon also read Mao's poetry and practiced using chopsticks.

Nixon had to do something to shore up buckling South Vietnam, and here Kissinger's strategy began to pay dividends. Having pulled all but about 60,000 American soldiers out of Southeast Asia (there had been more than half a million when he assumed office in 1969), the president had fewer weapons to wield on the ground. Not so from the air. In April 1972, he ordered massive strikes by B-52 bombers and, in May, the placing of mines in important North Vietnamese harbors. Kissinger, especially, worried that the attacks would destroy any chance for improved relations with China and the Soviet Union. The howls of protest expected from the Communist giants never came, however. Nixon flew to Moscow on May 22 for his meeting with Leonid Brezhnev, as planned.

The North Vietnamese felt betrayed by the welcome the Soviets extended to Nixon at the Moscow summit, and both the Russians and Chinese now pressed the North Vietnamese to talk with the U.S. Le Duc Tho, lead negotiator for North Vietnam, met secretly with Kissinger several times during the summer and fall; this time his country was prepared to soften some demands, such as requiring the resignation of South Vietnamese president Nguyen Van Thieu. But the talks stalled, and Nixon ordered additional airstrikes in late December—the so-called "Christmas bombing" that killed more than 1,600 civilians in and around Hanoi, the capital of North Vietnam. In early January, Henry Kissinger returned to the bargaining table in Paris. The final peace agreement was signed on January 27, 1973—one week after Nixon was inaugurated for his second term.

It wasn't, however, a victory for the United States—North Vietnamese troops were not even required to leave the South. The accord did preserve the existence of South Vietnam, a concession Communist negotiators had fought for years, allowing Nixon and Kissinger to claim (however questionably) that the initial purpose of U.S. involvement in the war was met. But once the American soldiers withdrew, North Vietnam continued its drive, defeating the South in 1975.

Besides helping end the Vietnam War, the triangular balance also provided Nixon and Kissinger with a way to curb the arms race. By the late 1960s, the superpowers boasted a dizzying array of nuclear weapons. Intercontinental ballistic missiles (ICBMs) dotted territories, submarine-launched ballistic missiles (SLBMs) prowled beneath the oceans, and long-range bombers idled in aircraft hangars ready to fly at a moment's notice. Additionally, the U.S. was developing multiple independently targetable reentry vehicles (MIRVs)—ballistic missiles fitted with two or more warheads, each capable of hitting different targets. Nixon also hoped to deploy ABMs—antiballistic missiles, designed to destroy incoming Soviet missiles.

The Americans wanted an arms agreement because the Soviets, while roughly equal with the United States in numbers of ICBMs and SLBMs, were producing both at

multiple independently targetable reentry vehicle (MIRV): (rhymes with "nerve") a ballistic missile that carries multiple nuclear warheads, with each one programmed to hit a different target. MIRVs allow an increase in firepower without the building of more rockets.

A submarine-launched ballistic missile, the Trident C-4, being tested at a military base in Florida

a much faster rate. The Soviets also wanted to deal. Although they were gaining ground in ICBMs and SLBMs, they lagged far behind in developing MIRVs and ABMs. This meant the United States, using MIRVs, could launch more warheads with fewer missiles than the Soviet Union. And with ABMs, the Americans presumably could survive a nuclear exchange while the Soviets would disappear in a giant fireball. A potential U.S.-China relationship only added to Soviet insecurity. For all these reasons, Soviet negotiators sat down in November 1969 with Kissinger's team at the Strategic Arms Limitation Talks (SALT) in Helsinki, Finland.

SALT I, signed in May 1972, left the two superpowers approximately equal strategically, although the U.S. had some advantages not covered by the treaty. ABM sites were limited to two per nation, a concession favored by the Soviets. At the same time, production of ICBMs and SLBMs were frozen at current levels, a move advantageous to the United States. Beyond these agreements, however, the accord failed to stop the arms buildup. Kissinger refused to ban MIRVs because they were the only way the United States could retain an edge with fewer missiles. As a result, the Soviets developed their own MIRVs. And long-range bombers weren't even discussed at the SALT talks. Kissinger would later try to introduce these issues with SALT II, but that treaty wasn't completed before he left office in January 1977.

Henry Kissinger with Soviet leaders Leonid Brezhnev (left of Kissinger, with medals on) and Andrei Gromyko (far left of photo) at SALT II, a second round of arms talks held in 1976

Elsewhere, Kissinger's balance of power succeeded in reducing Soviet influence in the Middle East. Since the 1960s, the Soviets had been supplying arms and military training to its Arab allies, including the armies of Egypt and Syria. Although in 1957 President Dwight Eisenhower and Secretary of State John Foster Dulles had vowed American support for any Mideast nation threatened by communist aggression, this had done little to stop Soviet arms shipments. Then, in June 1967, Israel attacked Egypt and Syria just as the two appeared poised for an invasion of the Jewish state. By the end of the "Six-Day War," Israel had captured the Sinai Peninsula from Egypt, the Golan Heights from Syria, and additional land from Jordan, including the west bank of the Jordan River and Jordan's portion of Jerusalem.

Humiliated, Moscow increased arms shipments to its two clients. Soviet supremacy in the region seemed likely until July 1972, when Egyptian president Anwar Sadat abruptly ended his nation's relationship with the Communist superpower. The Soviets, it seems, had refused to arm Egypt any further for fear of scuttling détente with the United States. Sadat retaliated by ordering the Soviet military instructors to leave.

Instead of reducing tension between the two superpowers, the crisis that followed included a threat of nuclear war. On October 6, 1973, the Jewish holy day of Yom Kippur, Egypt and Syria launched a surprise attack on Israel to regain land lost in 1967. They drove the Israelis back. Within two weeks, fierce Israeli counterattacks had pushed the Syrians back to their capital of Damascus and had encircled the Egyptians in the Sinai. On October 24, the Soviets threatened intervention to end the fighting. The warning was an obvious attempt to plant troops in the area, an event Kissinger and Nixon were prepared to resist by force.

Actually, with Richard Nixon so preoccupied with the Watergate scandal that ultimately would destroy his

presidency, Kissinger was conducting America's foreign policy almost alone. Without consulting Nixon, he placed U.S. nuclear forces on the highest alert short of war. Although Kissinger was now secretary of state (since August), his move was completely without precedent. Even Dulles had needed President Eisenhower's approval before threatening nuclear attack. In any event, Kissinger's bold gamble convinced the Soviet leaders to back down. From there, Sadat proposed talks to end the crisis. Israel agreed

Israeli leaders and soldiers take a victory tour of recently gained territory in east Jerusalem, one result of their success in the Six-Day War of 1967.

Watergate

The Watergate scandal forced President Richard Nixon to resign from office in August 1974. James McCord, Nixon's chief of security for his reelection committee, and several other men who had previously worked for Nixon had broken into the Washington, D.C., headquarters of the Democratic National Committee on June 17, 1972, in order to bug the phones. Many of Nixon's closest friends and advisors were mixed up in the Watergate burglary either directly or indirectly.

Although Nixon denied having any prior knowledge of the break-in, he tried to keep investigators from linking him and his aides to it. Other members of his administration also tried to cover up their involvement in the scandal.

The cover-up worked for a while, until some members of the administration began giving information to journalists and Congressional investigators. Although many of his aides were linked to the crime, Nixon at first appeared to be uninvolved. He was eventually forced to release some tapes of conversations recorded in his offices that incriminated him and led to his resignation.

The Watergate scandal takes its name from the office complex that housed the headquarters of the Democratic National Committee. Ever since Watergate, adding "-gate" to a noun has often been used as shorthand for many other government scandals.

G. Gordon Liddy, a strong Nixon supporter who worked for the Committee to Re-elect the President (CREEP), was the chief planner of the Watergate break-in.

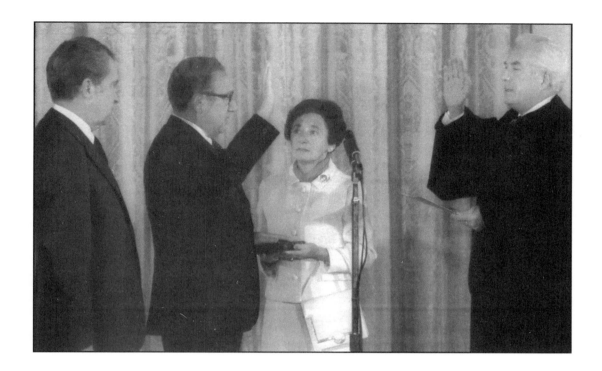

and the first Arab-Israeli peace conference followed. Once the crisis cooled, it became clear that Soviet credibility with the Arabs had withered.

Looking Forward

Long after Kissinger left office in January 1977, the multinational balance he nurtured continued to shape international relations. In 1979, President Jimmy Carter officially normalized diplomatic relations with China. Although the American-Chinese relationship worsened in the early 1980s, it recovered after President Ronald Reagan visited Beijing in April 1984. Reagan's renewal of détente with the Chinese was not lost on the Soviet Union as it struggled to keep pace with Reagan's massive arms buildup.

By then, relations between the Soviets and Americans had taken a nosedive. Moscow, sensing U.S. weakness in the wake of Vietnam, had tried to gain a foothold in

Few immigrants have had as much influence over U.S. foreign policy as Henry Kissinger, who would serve President Gerald Ford as well as President Nixon. Here Chief Justice Warren Burger swears Kissinger into office as secretary of state while Kissinger's mother, Paula, and Nixon look on.

Henry Kissinger (center) talks with three former secretaries of state: (left to right) Cyrus Vance (1917-2002), William Rogers (1913-2001), and Dean Rusk (1909-1994).

Africa in the mid-1970s. In October 1976, the Soviets signed a treaty of friendship with Angola. By 1978, Soviet advisors together with Cuban troops had propelled Ethiopia to victory over pro-American Somalia. While all this was unfolding, Colonel Muammar al-Qaddafi of Libya, who had assumed power in 1969, continued to use Soviet military and economic aid to undermine the stability of his pro-Western neighbors. Also souring the relationship was the Soviet invasion of Afghanistan in December 1979. Carter increased defense spending by five percent, limited grain shipments to the Soviet Union, and initiated a boy-cott of the 1980 Olympics set to open in Moscow the following summer. In addition, the president advised the U.S. Senate to wait to consider the SALT II treaty he had initialed just months earlier. As Carter left office in 1981, détente seemed dead.

It wasn't. As Carter, then Reagan, increased defense outlays, the Soviets were hard pressed to keep pace. By the mid-1980s, Soviet leader Mikhail Gorbachev realized his empire could no longer afford confrontation with the Americans and the Chinese. He strove to reduce tensions with both while attempting to open and modernize his own society. In the latter, he failed. Within seven years of his rise to power in March 1985, the Soviet Union disinte-grated, partly from being under the strain of four decades of superpower competition. It would be up to Reagan's successor to guide the world through the resulting chaos.

Henry Kissinger saw it all. Unlike former secretary of state Dean Acheson, Kissinger was not offered any unofficial advisory duties after he left office. Carter wanted no advice from a Republican secretary of state. Reagan was no more solicitous; he was vehemently anti-Soviet and had always thought that détente with the Soviet Union was misguided. Instead, Henry Kissinger taught part-time at Georgetown University in Washington and wrote his memoirs. In addi-tion, Kissinger regularly appeared on news programs to analyze world events of the day from his perspective as an elder statesman of American politics and foreign policy.

★ ★ *8* ★ ★

JAMES ADDISON BAKER III

The Persian Gulf War and the Global Coalition

Coalition-building was nothing new to James Baker. When George H. W. Bush ran for the U.S. Senate from Texas in 1970, Baker managed his close friend's campaign in the state's most populous county. Bush lost the race overall, but won convincingly among Harris County voters. When the two resumed their roles as candidate and campaign manager in 1980, Bush was challenging Ronald Reagan for the Republican presidential nomination. Bush, the underdog, lost the nomination, but Baker's fence-mending with the Reagan team got Bush the nod as Reagan's vice president. That enabled Bush to run for president in 1988 as the front-runner, a race he won with Baker's help as his campaign manager.

Now, in the wake of Iraq's lightning-quick invasion of Kuwait in August 1990, Baker was helping Bush craft what would be the greatest coalition of their public careers. The United States, seeking to arouse worldwide indignation against Saddam Hussein, Iraq's dictator, hoped to remove him from Kuwait with the help of as many countries as possible. Beneath the sands of Iraq, Kuwait, and Saudi Arabia—Saddam's likely next target—lay 40 percent of the world's known oil supply. Should the Iraqi tyrant gain control of this vital energy source, his naked aggression

James Baker (b. 1930) kept an international coalition together to fight off the Iraqi invasion of Kuwait, proving that the U.S. was willing to become involved in far-off conflicts if its interests were threatened.

might earn him world power. But could Baker and Bush unite traditional foes—for example, Western Europeans and Russians or Arabs and Israelis—to stop Saddam?

The Formative Years ─────────

James Addison (Jim) Baker III was born in Houston, Texas, on April 28, 1930, to James and Bonner Means Baker. James, a lawyer, and son Jim were very close, despite the fact that the elder Baker routinely doused his son with cold water whenever he overslept. But James's lessons of self-discipline slowly sank in. As Jim later recalled, "My father had always told me as I grew up, 'Prior preparation prevents poor performance.' The 'Five Ps,' as they were known, were drilled into my head at an early age, and I realized that careful preparation and hard work could take you a long way."

Like his father, Jim studied hard and attended the best schools. After attending a private elementary school in Houston, he went to an elite Pennsylvania boarding school. Jim spent his college years at New Jersey's Princeton University, graduating in 1952. Following two years in the U.S. Marine Corps, he entered the University of Texas Law School. It was the same school his father had gone through. "If you're going to practice law in Texas," James had told his son, "you go to the law school in Austin and make all the contacts you can. They'll pay off later." Getting to know people and making contacts was indeed a valuable lesson that would pay off for Jim Baker.

After graduating with honors from law school in 1957, Baker joined a notable Houston law firm. There he assisted one of the senior attorneys who, according to one of Baker's colleagues, "was a fantastic lawyer—the best I've seen at bringing parties locked in impossible conflicts together."

Baker met George Bush in the 1960s, and the two spent time together on the tennis courts of the Houston Country Club. Both were top-notch players, and they quickly became close friends, even pairing up to win doubles championships. Bush coaxed Baker into leaving his successful law practice for a career in politics when Bush ran for the U.S. Senate in 1970. Baker's wife, Mary Stuart (whom he had married in 1953), had recently died of cancer, and Bush thought Baker's helping run the campaign might take his friend's mind off her death. They lost the race, but forged a lasting political partnership.

When President Gerald Ford appointed Baker undersecretary of commerce in August 1975, it was likely the result of Bush's lobbying. Bush was Ford's envoy (diplomatic representative) to China at the time. After just nine months in the Commerce Department, Baker joined Ford's presidential campaign. The president was locked in a tight battle for the Republican nomination with Ronald Reagan and desperately needed someone who could garner the support of undecided Republican delegates. Baker succeeded, and Ford went on to face Democrat Jimmy Carter in the November election. With Baker managing the campaign, Ford almost pulled off the victory, despite Carter's big early lead and the stain of the Watergate scandal on the Republicans.

When Bush ran for president in 1980, he naturally chose close friend Jim Baker to run his campaign. They never made it past Reagan, who was favored from the beginning to gain the Republican nomination. Reagan did offer Bush the vice presidency, a fine consolation prize for which Baker deserved most of the credit; it was Baker who had convinced Bush not to antagonize Reagan too much during the primaries.

Baker next engineered the Reagan-Bush victory over Carter in the general election. Reagan reciprocated by naming Baker chief of staff. In the post, Baker controlled daily White House operations and was able to keep Bush "in the loop" on most major decisions.

Baker resigned from Reagan's staff to lead the Treasury Department in January 1985. He left the post in August 1988 amid high praise from the nation's press. While

James Baker thought of George H. W. Bush (b. 1924), the 41st president of the United States, as a brother and said that Bush was the one who first interested him in politics.

James Baker (right) and George Bush during the 1988 presidential campaign

running the Treasury Department, Baker had hammered out agreements with other industrial nations that stabilized currency exchange rates and staved off global recession. He succeeded despite the U.S.'s weakening economic power. "He understood the United States couldn't do things unilaterally as it had in the past," commented one economist. "But he still managed to assert leadership. He saw that the United States couldn't lead simply by making statements and having others follow; it had to lead by bringing others along." How had the treasury secretary managed this? "Baker," explained a journalist in August 1988, "made profitable use of what is perhaps his most formidable skill—his talent for negotiating and coalition-building."

In the Cabinet

When Bush became president in January 1989, he nominated James Baker as the 61st secretary of state of the

United States. From the beginning, their close friendship enabled them to run U.S. foreign policy with exceptional smoothness and effectiveness. Both excelled at cultivating personal relationships with congressional and foreign leaders.

As Baker settled into office, the long-standing need to block Soviet expansionism was waning. George Kennan had written in 1947 that a "policy of firm containment" would someday force a "gradual mellowing of Soviet power." Clearly this was now happening. Soviet leader Mikhail Gorbachev, frantically pursuing economic reform to keep his empire together, was downsizing his expensive military. A shift away from confrontation was not inevitable, however. Conservatives near Gorbachev hoped to reverse course. The situation was potentially explosive: "At a minimum America would have to contend with a very unstable international environment," Baker recalled, while, "In the worst case, we could see a cold war become a hot one."

As soon as it looked as if he might win the presidential race, George Bush asked James Baker to become his secretary of state. Baker accepted immediately, and the two friends worked together through most of Bush's four years in office.

A concentrated effort to dissuade the Soviets from further confrontation was needed. Strengthening the Western alliance was an important first step, and Baker worked to tighten economic and security ties to Europe and the Pacific region. At the same time, he engaged the Soviets directly on various issues. Eduard Shevardnadze, the Soviet foreign minister, grew to be a respected counterpart.

Baker's constructive dialogue with Shevardnadze mirrored Bush's with Gorbachev. This made the Soviets comfortable enough to continue withdrawing troops, tanks, and artillery from Eastern Europe. Bush responded in May 1989 by proposing cuts in NATO (North Atlantic Treaty Organization) forces in Western Europe. It appeared the two sides were no longer enemies.

James Baker with George Bush and Eduard Shevardnadze (center), the Soviet foreign minister, in September 1989

Just weeks later, on June 4, Chinese leaders cracked down on pro-democracy demonstrators gathered in Beijing's Tiananmen Square. In shaping the official U.S. response, Bush and Baker considered American domestic

politics as well as foreign. Most conservatives demanded a hard line against all communists, while liberals concentrated on China's abuse of human rights. A firm response would have appeased both groups while also warning Soviet hard-liners not to try a similar crackdown in Eastern Europe, but Bush and Baker chose more moderate economic sanctions. Above all, Bush and Baker reasoned, the U.S.-Chinese relationship had to survive not only for the benefit of American trade, but also to pressure the Soviet Union. As it turned out, the mild measure would pay off in another, unforeseen way.

As the end of 1989 approached, the Soviet grip on Eastern Europe continued to loosen as more reform governments rejected communism. Gorbachev renounced Soviet rule over East Germany in October, marking the first step toward eventual German reunification. A strong

At the order of the Chinese government, the army fired upon peaceful student demonstrators on June 4, 1989, in Tiananmen Square. Hundreds were killed. This photo—of one unarmed civilian confronting a column of tanks—came to symbolize China's ruthless suppression of dissent.

and united Germany terrified the Soviets—Adolf Hitler's invasion in World War II had killed millions—but they simply could no longer afford an empire. Ironically, Baker reassured them by promising that the U.S. military would not leave Europe. In November 1989, East Germany opened its borders for the first time since 1945, and the Soviets did nothing, despite still having 400,000 troops in the country.

On December 20, the United States invaded Panama to oust troublesome dictator Manuel Noriega. As Baker explained, the strongman's "corrupt and repressive military regime undermined our efforts both to promote democracy in the hemisphere and to combat narcotics trafficking," the latter in which Noriega was heavily involved. Even more worrisome was the status of the Panama Canal. Vital to American security since its opening in 1914, the waterway could not be allowed to fall into hostile hands. The success of the invasion went beyond removing Noriega, however. Baker felt it broke "the mind-set of the American people about the use of force in the post-Vietnam era. . . ."

Americans' willingness to flex their nation's military muscle was soon to be tested, as was the budding spirit of cooperation between the United States and the Soviet Union. On August 2, 1990, Iraq's Saddam Hussein, unable to repay the billions of dollars loaned him by Kuwait to finance his war with Iran from 1980 to 1988, invaded the defenseless country instead. This caused concern for the Bush team about where Saddam would move next. Conquest of neighboring Saudi Arabia, together with its other holdings, would give Iraq control of much of the world's known oil reserves.

Rather than confronting Saddam alone, the U.S. organized a large multinational force against him. Its strategy of gradually increasing pressure until Iraq cracked (diplomatic protests, then economic sanctions, then military force) could not succeed without aid from an international coalition. The key to the whole structure was the

Saddam Hussein's invasion of Kuwait would trigger a military response from the United States.

Soviet Union, Iraq's strongest ally and primary weapons supplier. If the Soviets refused to cut Saddam adrift, the Cold War could drag on. On the other hand, if the Soviets turned their back on Iraq, they would not only lose their primary client in the region, but also any remaining credibility with Arab nations.

George Bush with Mikhail Gorbachev, the Soviet president, in May 1990

In the end, Gorbachev chose cooperation instead of confrontation. The postwar goal of containing Soviet influence in the world was suddenly accomplished. On August 3, Shevardnadze stood with Baker and condemned Saddam's actions as "inconsistent with the principles of new political thinking and, in fact, with the civilized relations between nations."

With the Soviets in hand, Baker turned to the United Nations, under whose auspices the coalition would operate. Any of the five permanent members of the UN Security Council could block action by the international body.

The Bush team, including Baker (left), meets with Chinese diplomats in November 1990

With Soviet, British, and French support assured, only China worried Baker. (The U.S. was the fifth member.) As UN resolutions condemning the invasion and implementing economic sanctions were handed down, however, the Chinese did nothing. Although China surely had other reasons for approving the U.S.-led coalition, Bush's earlier moderation in the wake of the Tiananmen massacre certainly didn't hurt the U.S.'s case.

Having established "perm five" support, Baker turned his attention to tightening the economic screws. Saudi Arabia and Turkey were the greatest question marks here. Iraqi oil for export was Saddam Hussein's greatest source of revenue, and pipelines carrying it traversed both of these nations. The Saudis readily agreed to block the flow. Turkey also cooperated, despite the potential loss of perhaps $2.5 billion in pipeline payments. To offset the loss, Baker arranged for the Turks to receive loans from the World Bank.

If economic sanctions failed, the coalition would fight. Baker's primary challenge was to finance America's share of the military effort, far and away the greatest. A generation earlier, the United States might have taken financial responsibility for the effort. Since 1969, however, the last year its budget had been in balance, the U.S. had needed to borrow money to pay its bills. By 1986, it had accumulated more debt than any other nation. Clearly, to finance the type of overwhelming campaign necessary to defeat Iraq before international and American public support eroded, the United States would need help. Fortunately, the Saudis and Kuwaitis were willing to fund most of the coalition's cost. Chancellor Helmut Kohl of West Germany and Prime Minister Toshiki Kaifu of Japan, both on the best of terms with Baker and Bush, also pledged assistance.

Besides Saudi Arabia and Kuwait, other nations in the Middle East had to support the coalition if Iraq were to be isolated. Most Arab leaders, like Presidents Hosni Mubarak of Egypt and Hafiz al-Assad of Syria, supplied troops. Others were less willing to cross Saddam. King Hussein of Jordan refused to condemn the Iraqi invasion, even telling Prime Minister Margaret Thatcher of the United Kingdom, "the Kuwaitis had it coming." President Ali Abdullah Saleh of Yemen, who hated the Saudis, did his best to torpedo the coalition and instructed his UN representative to vote against the resolution of January 1991 authorizing force.

The region's real wild card was Israel. Saddam, who never masked his desire for Israel's destruction, might provoke the Jewish state to violence. If this happened, Arab public support for the coalition might evaporate, because most of the Arabs did not want to support Israel. On January 16, Iraqi missiles began hitting Israel in response to the opening of American air attacks. Although Israeli prime minister Yitzhak Shamir realized that retaliation was counterproductive, he could not withstand demands from

Members of Bush's cabinet meet on January 15, 1991. The U.S.-led coalition launched air and missile attacks on Iraq the following day.

Patriot missile: a surface-to-air missile (a missile launched from land or sea against a target in the air) that uses radar to find its target

members of his cabinet for immediate retribution. Bush and Baker had no choice but to refuse Shamir the identification codes used by coalition jets. Without the codes, Israeli planes could have been destroyed before they ever reached Iraq. In typical Bush-Baker fashion, however, they helped Shamir calm his opposition in Israel by doubling the number of American "Patriot" missiles protecting Israeli cities.

As Baker juggled efforts to maintain support within the alliance and his own country, American-dominated air and ground forces devastated Saddam's army in Operation Desert Storm. On February 27, on the heels of Kuwait's liberation from Iraqi control, Bush declared a cease-fire. The global coalition had succeeded in accomplishing its objectives.

Looking Forward

James Baker continued as secretary of state until August 1992, when he resigned to act as Bush's chief of staff and to run the last of his friend's political campaigns, a reelection bid that would fail in November. When the Bush administration left office in January 1993, Baker became honorary chairman of the James A. Baker III Institute for Public Policy at Rice University in Houston. He then became senior partner at Baker & Botts, the law firm to which his great-grandfather lent his name in 1872, and continued to speak and write about foreign policy issues.

Baker's coalition-building as secretary of state kept U.S. foreign policy going in the direction that Dean Acheson had sent it in when he wrote the Truman Doctrine. Baker secured ties with countries around the world, including cementing a friendly relationship with Russia as the Soviet Union broke up. This pushed the U.S. into even further economic and military interdependence with the rest of the world. Most importantly, the success of the Gulf War—the first major war since the Vietnam War—and Baker's coalition showed that the U.S. was still willing to become involved and even use military force wherever its global interests were threatened.

U.S. forces in Kuwait City during the Gulf War

★ ★ ★ ★

EPILOGUE

Responding to Terrorism

In 1991, General Colin Powell probably never imagined that, one decade later, he would be secretary of state fighting a very different battle than the Persian Gulf War. Powell had been in office less than nine months when Arab terrorists hijacked four airplanes on September 11, 2001, and used them to kill 3,000 people on U.S. soil. Powell found himself faced with one of the toughest diplomatic challenges in American history—and using coalition building methods similar to those of former secretary of state James Baker.

After the attacks on New York and Washington, U.S. intelligence quickly determined that the hijackers belonged to al-Qaeda, a worldwide terrorist organization based in the central-Asian country of Afghanistan. Working closely with President George W. Bush, Powell informed the rulers of Afghanistan, the Islamic fundamentalist Taliban, that their cooperation in bringing al-Qaeda to justice was expected. By the time it became clear that the Taliban would not help, Powell had lined up most of the world's leaders behind the U.S. goal of rooting out al-Qaeda—and the Taliban—by military force.

His efforts would become critical components of what would come to be known as the Bush Doctrine, which the president outlined in a speech before a joint session of Congress on September 20. "Either you are with us, or

Colin Powell (b. 1937), chairman of the joint chiefs of staff (America's top military official) under George Bush and secretary of state under George W. Bush, said of U.S. foreign policy in 2001, "America stands ready to help any country that wishes to join the democratic world."

151

you are with the terrorists," stated Bush. "From this day forward, any nation that continues to harbor or support terrorism will be regarded by the United States as a hostile regime."

For the U.S. to strike al-Qaeda effectively, however, Afghanistan's neighbors would have to be persuaded to lend their assistance. Pakistan, which U.S. leaders had shunned for years, shared the longest border with Afghanistan. Its military ruler, General Pervez Musharraf, had in fact supported the Taliban, and many Pakistanis were sympathetic to the Islamic regime. Afghanistan's other neighbors, including newly independent countries that had formerly been part of the Soviet Union, also had predominantly Muslim populations, among whom were many people who sympathized with the Taliban. In addition, the Russians, who had lost a bitter war in Afghanistan in the 1980s, still considered the region to be well within their sphere of influence.

Remarkably, by combining tough talk, financial pressure or incentives, and the moral outrage that arose from the terrorists' carnage, Bush and Powell succeeded in gaining the cooperation they needed. U.S. forces would be

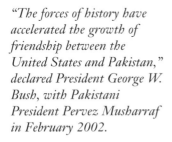

"The forces of history have accelerated the growth of friendship between the United States and Pakistan," declared President George W. Bush, with Pakistani President Pervez Musharraf in February 2002.

Secretary of State Colin Powell shakes hands on September 28, 2001, with Yerlan Idrisov, foreign minister of the Republic of Kazakhstan. This country, home to millions of Muslims and once a part of the Soviet Union, agreed to help in the war against terrorism.

allowed to base military operations into Afghanistan from neighboring countries and fly through their air space. With the Russians permitting American soldiers on what had only a few years before been Soviet soil, the Cold War was certainly over. In a matter of weeks, the U.S. and its anti-Taliban Afghan allies removed the Taliban from power and forced the al-Qaeda terrorists who were neither killed nor captured to flee for their lives. A new regime, under the leadership of Afghan tribal chief Hamid Karzai, was established in Kabul, the capital of Afghanistan.

This far from ended the terrorist threat to the United States posed by al-Qaeda and like-minded groups, but it did mark the beginning of the country's war against terrorism. To win the war, American leaders warned, would require years of persistence and patience. The secretaries of state directing U.S. diplomacy would need to demonstrate the same ingenuity, courage, and vision that previous secretaries have employed in times of crisis.

Madeleine Korbel Albright (b. 1937) served as secretary of state—the first woman to ever hold the position—under President Bill Clinton from 1997 to 2001. An international affairs professor, Albright advised several Democratic presidential candidates on foreign policy, including Clinton. After he won election in 1992, Clinton appointed Albright as U.S. representative to the United Nations, where she served until selected as secretary of state.

SECRETARIES OF STATE

	date of appointment	president(s) served
Thomas Jefferson	March 22, 1789	Washington
Edmund Randolph	January 2, 1794	Washington
Timothy Pickering	December 10, 1795	Washington, Adams
John Marshall	June 6, 1800	Adams
James Madison	May 2, 1801	Jefferson
Robert Smith	March 6, 1809	Madison
James Monroe	April 2, 1811	Madison
John Quincy Adams	March 5, 1817	Monroe
Henry Clay	March 7, 1825	J. Q. Adams
Martin Van Buren	March 6, 1829	Jackson
Edward Livingston	May 24, 1831	Jackson
Louis McLane	May 29, 1833	Jackson
John Forsyth	June 27, 1834	Jackson, Van Buren
Daniel Webster*	March 5, 1841	Harrison, Tyler
Abel P. Upshur	July 24, 1843	Tyler
John C. Calhoun	March 6, 1844	Tyler, Polk
James Buchanan	March 7, 1845	Polk, Taylor
John M. Clayton	March 7, 1849	Taylor, Fillmore
Daniel Webster*	July 22, 1850	Fillmore
Edward Everett	November 6, 1852	Fillmore
William L. Marcy	March 7, 1853	Pierce, Buchanan
Lewis Cass	March 6, 1857	Buchanan
Jeremiah S. Black	December 17, 1860	Buchanan, Lincoln
William H. Seward	March 5, 1861	Lincoln, Johnson
Elihu B. Washburne	March 5, 1869	Grant
Hamilton Fish	March 11, 1869	Grant, Hayes
William M. Evarts	March 12, 1877	Hayes, Garfield
James G. Blaine*	March 5, 1881	Garfield, Arthur
Frederick T. Frelinghuysen	February 12, 1881	Arthur, Cleveland
Thomas F. Bayard	March 6, 1885	Cleveland, Harrison
James G. Blaine*	March 5, 1889	Harrison
John W. Foster	June 29, 1892	Harrison
Walter Q. Gresham	March 6, 1893	Cleveland
Richard Olney	June 8, 1895	Cleveland, McKinley
John Sherman	March 5, 1897	McKinley

William R. Day	April 26, 1898	McKinley
John Hay	September 20, 1898	McKinley, T. Roosevelt
Elihu Root	July 7, 1905	T. Roosevelt
Robert Bacon	January 27, 1909	T. Roosevelt, Taft
Philander C. Knox	March 5, 1909	Taft, Wilson
William Jennings Bryan	March 5, 1913	Wilson
Robert Lansing	June 23, 1915	Wilson
Bainbridge Colby	March 22, 1920	Wilson
Charles Evans Hughes	March 4, 1921	Harding, Coolidge
Frank B. Kellogg	February 16, 1925	Coolidge, Hoover
Henry Lewis Stimson	March 5, 1929	Hoover
Cordell Hull	March 4, 1933	FDR
Edward R. Stettinius Jr.	November 30, 1944	FDR, Truman
James F. Byrnes	July 2, 1945	Truman
George C. Marshall	January 8, 1947	Truman
Dean G. Acheson	January 19, 1949	Truman
John Foster Dulles	January 21, 1953	Eisenhower
Christian A. Herter	April 21, 1959	Eisenhower
Dean Rusk	January 21, 1961	Kennedy, Johnson
William P. Rogers	January 21, 1969	Nixon
Henry A. Kissinger	September 21, 1973	Nixon, Ford
Cyrus Vance	January 21, 1977	Carter
Edmund S. Muskie	May 8, 1980	Carter
Alexander M. Haig Jr.	January 22, 1981	Reagan
George P. Shultz	July 16, 1982	Reagan
James A. Baker III	January 25, 1989	Bush
Lawrence S. Eagleburger	December 8, 1992	Bush
Warren M. Christopher	January 20, 1993	Clinton
Madeleine K. Albright	January 17, 1997	Clinton
Colin L. Powell	January 20, 2001	G. W. Bush

*served in the same position twice

GLOSSARY

annexation: the making of a territory into part of an existing state or nation

antiballistic missile (ABM): a defensive weapon designed to destroy a ballistic missile in the air

arbitration: a means of solving a conflict between two or more nations in which the differences are presented to an impartial court

artillery: large-caliber weapons, such as cannons or missile launchers; also the branch of the army that specializes in using these weapons

ballistic missile: a rocket that is allowed to fall freely, following a path like a thrown ball, after being launched and reaching a predetermined location under rocket power; *see also* **intercontinental ballistic missile**

bar exam: a licensing test lawyers must pass in order to practice before the bar, or court

battleship: one of the largest warships, with the most guns and heaviest armor; *see also* **capital ships**

capital ships: the biggest and heaviest of the warships, including battleships and battle cruisers, which carry guns larger than eight inches; *see also* **battleship**

charge d'affaires: diplomat who temporarily heads a legation that is waiting for a replacement minister; *see also* **legation**

communism: a theoretical political and economic system in which all property is held in common. When capitalized, it refers to a specific, historical system of government in which all property is owned by the totalitarian state.

de facto: a Latin phrase that means actually or in fact, but not officially or in name

détente: (day-TAHNT) a policy of relaxing tensions between two nations through increased contact and negotiations, especially in reference to relations between the United States and the Soviet Union in the 1970s and 1980s

diplomat: a person appointed to represent his or her government in relations with the governments of other nations

embassy: a diplomatic establishment in a foreign country in which an ambassador works to conduct relations with that country

envoy: a diplomatic representative ranking between an ambassador and a resident minister

fascism: a political philosophy that exalts the state above the individual and is characterized by a centralized government led by a dictator, economic and social controls, and brutal suppression of opposition

Federalist: a member or supporter of the Federalist Party, an American political party formed in 1787, which advocated a strong federal government and adoption of the Constitution by the states

Holy Alliance: an organization of European monarchs formed by Alexander I of Russia, Francis I of Austria, and Frederick William III of Prussia in 1815. Although the stated mission of the alliance was to promote the use of Christian ideas in national affairs, the leaders participating in the alliance mostly wanted to put down rebellions and maintain their power as monarchs.

inflation: a continuous rise in prices caused by an increase of available currency and credit beyond what the available goods and services can sustain

insurgents: people who rebel by force against a particular authority, especially a government

intercontinental ballistic missile (ICBM): a ballistic missile that is launched into the atmosphere to give it enough range (over 4,000 miles) to target other continents

internationalism: a foreign policy that seeks involvement with other countries through economic cooperation and political influence

international law: a loose set of guidelines that are generally accepted among nations as applying to their relations with each other

isolationism: a foreign policy that avoids interfering in the affairs of other countries unless the interests of one's own nation are directly threatened

joint chiefs of staff (JCS): the group of military advisors to the president that is made up of the chiefs of the army, navy, and air force, as well as the commandant of the Marines. The chairman of the joint chiefs of staff is considered America's top military leader.

joint session: a special session of Congress in which both the Senate and the House of Representatives meet in one place

legation: a diplomatic establishment, with a rank lower than an embassy

minister: a diplomat ranking just below an ambassador; *see also* **diplomat**

multiple independently targetable reentry vehicle (MIRV): (rhymes with "nerve") a ballistic missile that carries multiple nuclear warheads, each warhead programmed to hit a different target. MIRVs allow an increase in firepower without the building of more rockets.

nationalism: devotion to one's nation to the extent that the nation is more important than the individual

partisan: a devoted and fervent supporter of a party or cause, often used in regard to political parties

Patriot missile: a surface-to-air missile (a missile launched from land or sea against a target in the air) that uses radar to find its target

read law: to serve an apprenticeship under a lawyer, in order to learn to become a lawyer

reparations: compensation paid by one nation to a nation it has done injury to or damaged in some way, usually during war

republican: of or relating to a nation that has a political system in which a body of citizens elects representatives who are responsible to them

trade deficit: an imbalance in trade in which imports are larger than exports, so that a nation is in debt

tribunal: a judicial court or a committee appointed to resolve a dispute

SOURCE NOTES

Quoted passages are noted by page and order of citation.

Introduction

p. 7 (first): Warren I. Cohen, ed., *The Cambridge History of American Foreign Relations*, vol. 1 (New York: Cambridge University Press, 1993), 21-22.

p. 7 (second and third): Thomas G. Paterson, ed., *Major Problems in American Foreign Policy: Documents and Essays*, vol. 1 (Lexington, Mass.: Heath, 1978), 47.

pp. 7-8: Paterson, *Major Problems*, vol. 1, 88.

p. 8 (first and second): Paterson, *Major Problems*, vol. 1, 88.

p. 8 (third): Merrill D. Peterson, *Thomas Jefferson and the New Nation* (London: Oxford University Press, 1970), 658.

p. 8 (fourth): Paterson, *Major Problems*, vol. 1, 88.

p. 9: Paterson, *Major Problems*, vol. 1, 3.

Chapter One: John Quincy Adams

p. 13 (first): Samuel Flagg Bemis, *John Quincy Adams and the Foundations of American Foreign Policy* (Westport, Conn.: Greenwood, 1949), 176-177.

p. 13 (second and third): Bemis, *John Quincy Adams*, 177.

p. 15: Bemis, *John Quincy Adams*, 36.

p. 17 (first): Bemis, *John Quincy Adams*, 63.

p. 17 (second): Bemis, *John Quincy Adams*, 89.

p. 25: Bemis, *John Quincy Adams*, 391.

pp. 25-26: Bemis, *John Quincy Adams*, 392.

p. 26: Bemis, *John Quincy Adams*, 392.

Chapter Two: William Henry Seward

p. 29 (first): Glyndon G. Van Deusen, *William Henry Seward* (New York: Oxford University Press, 1967), 106.

p. 29 (second and third): Robert L. Beisner, *From the Old Diplomacy to the New* (Arlington Heights, Ill.: Harlan Davidson, 1986), 45.

p. 29 (fourth and fifth): Van Deusen, *William Henry Seward*, 207.

p. 34 (first): John M. Taylor, *William Henry Seward* (Washington, D.C.: Brassey's, 1991), 151.

p. 34 (second): Taylor, *William Henry Seward*, 178.

Chapter Three: John Hay

p. 45: Tyler Dennett, *John Hay* (Port Washington, N.Y.: Kennikat, 1933), 52.

p. 46 (first): Howard I. Kushner and Anne Hummel Sherrill, *John Milton Hay* (Boston: Twayne, 1977), 20.

p. 46 (second): Dennett, *John Hay*, 22.

p. 46 (third): Kenton J. Clymer, *John Hay: The Gentleman as Diplomat* (Ann Arbor, Mich.: University of Michigan Press, 1975), 32.

p. 47 (both): Clymer, *The Gentleman as Diplomat*, 33.

p. 49 (first): Dennett, *John Hay*, 153.

p. 49 (second): Beisner, *From the Old Diplomacy to the New*, 120-121.

p. 50 (first): Clymer, *The Gentleman as Diplomat*, 104.

p. 50 (second): Kushner and Sherrill, *John Milton Hay*, 85.

p. 51 (first): Clymer, *The Gentleman as Diplomat*, 120.

p. 51 (second): Clymer, *The Gentleman as Diplomat*, 121.

p. 51 (third and fourth): Thomas G. Paterson, J. Garry Clifford, and Kenneth J. Hagan, *American Foreign Policy: A History Since 1895* (Lexington, Mass.: Heath, 1995), 15.

p. 52 (first): Clymer, *The Gentleman as Diplomat*, 120.

p. 52 (second): Paterson, *Major Problems*, vol. 1, 276.

p. 53: Clymer, *The Gentleman as Diplomat*, 122.

p. 59 (all): Paterson, *Major Problems*, vol. 1, 420.

Chapter Four: Charles Evans Hughes

p. 63 (first): Merlo J. Pusey, *Charles Evans Hughes,* vol. 1 (New York: Macmillan, 1951), 5.

p. 63 (second): Betty Glad, *Charles Evans Hughes and the Illusions of Innocence* (Urbana, Ill.: University of Illinois Press, 1966), 13.

p. 64: Glad, *Illusions of Innocence*, 37.

p. 65: Glad, *Illusions of Innocence*, 91.

p. 68 (first): Glad, *Illusions of Innocence*, 89.

p. 68 (second): Glad, *Illusions of Innocence*, 169.

p. 71: Glad, *Illusions of Innocence*, 270.

p. 74 (first): Glad, *Illusions of Innocence*, 279.

p. 74 (second and third): Glad, *Illusions of Innocence*, 320.

p. 75: Pusey, *Charles Evans Hughes*, vol. 2, 614.

Chapter Five: Dean Acheson

p. 77 (all): James Chace, *Acheson* (New York: Simon and Schuster, 1998), 78.

p. 78 (first): Chace, *Acheson*, 22.

p. 78 (second): Chace, *Acheson*, 34.

p. 79: Chace, *Acheson*, 36.

p. 80 (first): Chace, *Acheson*, 45.

p. 80 (second and third): Chace, *Acheson*, 47.

p. 83: Chace, *Acheson*, 105.

p. 84-85: George F. Kennan, *Memoirs: 1925-1950* (Boston: Little, Brown, 1967), 549.

p. 85 (first): Kennan, *Memoirs*, 550.

p. 85 (second and third): Kennan, *Memoirs*, 557.

p. 86 (first): Chace, *Acheson*, 146.

p. 86 (second and third): Paterson, *Major Problems*, vol. 2, 291.

p. 87 (all): Chace, *Acheson*, 166.

p. 88 (all): Chace, *Acheson*, 166-168.

p. 89 (first): Chace, *Acheson*, 168.

p. 89 (second and third): Dean Acheson, *Present at the Creation: My Years in the State Department* (New York: Norton, 1969), 229.

p. 89 (fourth and fifth): Kennan, *Memoirs*, 359.

p. 92: Chace, *Acheson*, 279.

p. 94: Foster Rhea Dulles, *America's Rise to World Power: 1898-1954* (New York: Harper & Row, 1963), 231.

Chapter Six: John Foster Dulles

p. 101 (first): Michael A. Guhin, *John Foster Dulles: A Statesman and His Times* (New York: Columbia University Press, 1972), 39.

p. 101 (second): Guhin, *A Statesman and His Times*, 47.

p. 101 (third): Guhin, *A Statesman and His Times*, 48.

p. 103 (first): Guhin, *A Statesman and His Times*, 78.

p. 103 (second, third, and fourth): Guhin, *A Statesman and His Times*, 75.

p. 104: Guhin, *A Statesman and His Times*, 132.

p. 105 (all): Guhin, *A Statesman and His Times*, 140.

p. 106 (first and second): Townsend Hoopes, *The Devil and John Foster Dulles* (Boston: Little, Brown, 1973), 127.

p. 106 (third): Hoopes, *The Devil and John Foster Dulles*, 131.

p. 106 (fourth): Hoopes, *The Devil and John Foster Dulles*, 127.

p. 106 (fifth): Hoopes, *The Devil and John Foster Dulles*, 126.

p. 107: Guhin, *A Statesman and His Times*, 193.

p. 108: Hoopes, *The Devil and John Foster Dulles*, 127.

p. 109 (both): Hoopes, *The Devil and John Foster Dulles*, 161.

p. 110 (both): Hoopes, *The Devil and John Foster Dulles*, 161.

p. 112 (first): Paterson, Clifford, and Hagan, *American Foreign Policy*, 348.

p. 112 (second and third): John Lewis Gaddis, *Strategies of Containment* (New York: Oxford University Press, 1982), 137.

p. 113 (all): Hoopes, *The Devil and John Foster Dulles*, 277.

pp. 113-114: Dwight D. Eisenhower, *The White House Years: A Personal Account* (New York: Doubleday, 1963), 483.

p. 114 (first): Hoopes, *The Devil and John Foster Dulles*, 450.

p. 114 (second): Hoopes, *The Devil and John Foster Dulles*, 452.

Chapter Seven: Henry Kissinger

p. 118: Walter Isaacson, *Kissinger* (New York: Simon and Schuster, 1992), 27.

Chapter Eight: James Baker

p. 138 (first): James A. Baker, *The Politics of Diplomacy: Revolution, War, and Peace, 1989-1992* (New York: G. P. Putnam's Sons, 1995), 134.

p. 138 (second): "The Tactician," *The New Yorker*, May 7, 1990, 58.

p. 138 (third): "The Tactician," 62.

p. 140 (both): Paul Blustein, "James Baker Will Be a Tough Act to Follow," *Washington Post National Weekly Edition*, August 8-14, 1988, 21-22.

p. 141 (first and second): Chace, *Acheson*, 186.

p. 141 (third): Baker, *The Politics of Diplomacy*, 41.

p. 144 (first): Baker, *The Politics of Diplomacy*, 178.

p. 144 (second): Baker, *The Politics of Diplomacy*, 194.

p. 145: Baker, *The Politics of Diplomacy*, 2.

p. 147: George Bush and Brent Scowcroft, *A World Transformed* (New York: Knopf, 1998), 320.

Epilogue

p. 151 (caption): "Secretary of State Colin L. Powell." http://www.state.gov/secretary, cited April 4, 2001.

pp. 151-152: George W. Bush, Address to a Joint Session of Congress and the American people (U.S. Capitol, September 20, 2001), online at http://www.white-house.gov/news/releases/2001/09/20010920-8.html.

p. 152: George W. Bush, Address to the Media (Cross Hall, February 13, 2002), online at http://www.whitehouse.gov/president/worldunites/03.html.

BIBLIOGRAPHY

Acheson, Dean. *Present at the Creation: My Years in the State Department.* New York: Norton, 1969.

Baker, James A., III. *The Politics of Diplomacy: Revolution, War, and Peace, 1989-1992.* New York: G. P. Putnam's Sons, 1995.

Beisner, Robert L. *From the Old Diplomacy to the New.* Arlington Heights, Ill.: Harlan Davidson, 1986.

Bemis, Samuel Flagg. *John Quincy Adams and the Foundations of American Foreign Policy.* Westport, Conn.: Greenwood, 1949.

Blustein, Paul. "James Baker Will Be a Tough Act to Follow." *Washington Post National Weekly Edition*, August 8-14, 1988.

Bush, George, and Brent Scowcroft. *A World Transformed.* New York: Knopf, 1998.

Chace, James. *Acheson.* New York: Simon and Schuster, 1998.

Clymer, Kenton J. *John Hay: The Gentleman as Diplomat.* Ann Arbor, Mich.: University of Michigan Press, 1975.

Cohen, Roger. "Dependent on U.S. Now, Europe Vows Defense Push." *New York Times*, May 12, 1999.

Cohen, Warren I. *Dean Rusk.* Totowa, N.J.: Cooper Square, 1980.

———, ed. *The Cambridge History of American Foreign Relations.* 4 vols. New York: Cambridge University Press, 1993.

Crossette, Barbara. "China and Others Reject Pleas That the U.N. Halt Civil Wars." *New York Times*, September 23, 1999.

Current, Richard N., T. Harry Williams, Frank Freidel, and Alan Brinkley. *American History: to 1877.* New York: Knopf, 1987.

Dennett, Tyler. *John Hay.* Port Washington, N.Y.: Kennikat, 1933.

Dulles, Foster Rhea. *America's Rise to World Power: 1898-1954.* New York: Harper & Row, 1963.

Eisenhower, Dwight D. *The White House Years: A Personal Account.* New York: Doubleday, 1963.

Elliot, Michael. "Europe Starts to Get Serious." *Newsweek*, December 14, 1998.

Gaddis, John Lewis. *Strategies of Containment*. New York: Oxford University Press, 1982.

Glad, Betty. *Charles Evans Hughes and the Illusions of Innocence*. Urbana, Ill.: University of Illinois Press, 1966.

Glad, Paul W., ed. *William Jennings Bryan*. New York: Hill and Wang, 1968.

Guhin, Michael A. *John Foster Dulles: A Statesman and His Times*. New York: Columbia University Press, 1972.

Halberstam, David. *The Best and the Brightest*. New York: Random House, 1992.

Hodgson, Godfrey. *The Colonel: The Life and Wars of Henry Stimson, 1867-1950*. New York: Knopf, 1990.

Hoopes, Townsend. *The Devil and John Foster Dulles*. Boston: Little, Brown, 1973.

Isaacson, Walter. *Kissinger*. New York: Simon and Schuster, 1992.

Kagan, Donald, Steven Ozment, and Frank M. Turner. *The Western Heritage: Volume II, since 1648*. New York: Macmillan, 1987.

Karnow, Stanley. *Vietnam: A History*. New York: Penguin, 1983.

Kennan, George F. *Memoirs: 1925-1950*. Boston: Little, Brown, 1967.

Ketcham, Ralph. *James Madison*. New York: Macmillan, 1971.

Keylor, William R. *The Twentieth Century World*. New York: Oxford University Press, 1992.

Kissinger, Henry. *Diplomacy*. New York: Simon and Schuster, 1994.

———. *White House Years*. Boston: Little, Brown, 1979.

———. *A World Restored: Metternich, Castlereagh, and the Problems of Peace*. Boston: Houghton Mifflin, 1957.

———. *Years of Upheaval*. Boston: Little, Brown, 1982.

Kushner, Howard I., and Anne Hummel Sherrill. *John Milton Hay*. Boston: Twayne, 1977.

Marks, Frederick W., III. *Power and Peace: The Diplomacy of John Foster Dulles*. Westport, Conn.: Praeger, 1993.

Nevins, Allan, ed. *The Diary of John Quincy Adams*. New York: Longmans, Green, 1928.

Paterson, Thomas G., ed. *Major Problems in American Foreign Policy: Documents and Essays*. 2 vols. Lexington, Mass.: Heath, 1978.

Paterson, Thomas G., J. Garry Clifford, and Kenneth J. Hagan. *American Foreign Policy: A History Since 1895*. Lexington, Mass.: Heath, 1995.

Perkins, Dexter. *Charles Evans Hughes and American Democratic Statesmanship*. Westport, Conn.: Greenwood, 1956.

Peterson, Merrill D. *Thomas Jefferson and the New Nation*. London: Oxford University Press, 1970.

Pusey, Merlo J. *Charles Evans Hughes*. 2 vols. New York: Macmillan, 1951.

Rich, Norman. *Great Power Diplomacy: 1814-1914*. New York: McGraw-Hill, 1992.

Rosenberg, Emily S. *Spreading the American Dream*. New York: Hill and Wang, 1982.

Rusk, Dean. *As I Saw It*. New York: Norton, 1990.

Russell, Francis. *The Shadow of Blooming Grove: Warren G. Harding and His Times*. New York: McGraw-Hill, 1968.

"Secretary of State Colin L. Powell." http://www.state.gov/secretary, cited April 4, 2001.

Sprout, Harold and Margaret. *The Rise of American Naval Power, 1776-1918*. Annapolis, Md.: Naval Institute Press, 1966.

"The Tactician." *The New Yorker*, May 7, 1990.

Taylor, John M. *William Henry Seward*. Washington, D.C.: Brassey's, 1991.

Van Deusen, Glyndon G. *William Henry Seward*. New York: Oxford University Press, 1967.

Walker, Martin. *The Cold War: A History*. New York: Holt, 1993.

INDEX

Acheson, Dean, 114; as advisor to Kennedy and Johnson, 94-95; anti-Soviet measures of, 83, 87-91; as assistant secretary of state, 82-83; death of, 95; as delegate to Bretton Woods conference, 82-83; early years of, 78; influenced by Brandeis, Frankfurter, and Holmes, 79-80; as secretary of state, 10-11, 91-92, 93, 135; Truman Doctrine written by, 10, 77, 88-89, 92, 94, 149; as undersecretary of state, 83-91; as undersecretary of treasury, 81-82

Acheson, Edward (father), 78

Acheson, Eleanor Gooderham (mother), 78

Adams, Abigail (mother), 14

Adams, Henry (grandson), 53

Adams, John (father), 7, 13, 14, 15, 17

Adams, John Quincy, 53, 59; death of, 27, 29; as diplomat, 13, 15, 17, 18, 20; early years of, 13-15; as isolationist, 10, 15, 19; Monroe Doctrine written by, 10, 13, 25, 93-94; opposition of, to slavery, 26, 29; as president, 26, 30, 33; as secretary of state, 10, 13, 21-26, 75; as U.S. senator, 18; U.S. territory gained by, 21-24

Afghanistan, 134, 151, 152, 153

Alabama, 38, 40

Alaska, 24, 41

Albright, Madeleine, 154

Alexander I (tsar of Russia), 13, 24, 25

Allies, 67, 100, 103, 118, 123

al-Qaeda, 151, 152, 153

Anglo-Saxonism, 50-51

Angola, 134

antiballistic missiles (ABMs), 127, 128, 129

Antimason Party, 33

anti-Semitism, 117-118

Arabs, 130, 133, 138, 145, 147, 151

arms race, 127-128, 134, 135

Army, U.S., 9, 77

al-Assad, Hafiz, 147

atomic bomb, 11, 105, 107-108, 110, 113. *See also* nuclear weapons

Baker, Bonner Means (mother), 138

Baker, James (father), 138

Baker, James Addison, III: early years of, 138; Gulf War coalition created by, 137, 145-148, 149, 151; as lawyer, 138, 139, 149; relationship of, with Bush, 137, 138-139, 140-141, 149; as secretary of state, 11, 137, 140-149; as secretary of treasury, 139-140; and U.S. relations with Soviet Union, 141-142

Baker, Mary Stuart (wife), 139

balance of power, 117, 120-121, 123, 125, 126, 127, 130

Berlin Blockade, 91

Berlin Conference, 100

Bonaparte, Napoleon, 13, 16, 18-19, 20, 23, 24, 120

Booth, John Wilkes, 38, 39

Boxer Rebellion, 58-59

Brandeis, Louis, 80

Bretton Woods conference, 82-83

Brezhnev, Leonid, 126, 129

Brooks Island, 42

Brussels Defense Pact, 90

Bunker Hill, Battle of, 14

Burger, Warren, 133

Bush, George, 137-139, 140-141, 142, 143, 145, 146, 147, 148, 149, 151

Eisenhower, Dwight, 107, 109, 110, 112, 113-114, 115, 130, 131

Emancipation Proclamation, 36

Ethiopia, 134

Federalists, 17, 18, 33

Ferdinand Maximilian, 39, 40

Five-Power Treaty, 70-71, 73, 74, 75

Florida, 21, 23-24

Ford, Gerald, 133, 139

Foster, John W., 97, 98

France, 9, 14, 17, 39, 54, 55, 66, 90, 100, 103; Bonaparte as ruler of, 13, 16, 18, 20, 24; navy of, 71, 73; as nuclear power, 117; revolution in, 15, 16, 24; during U.S. Civil War, 34, 35-36; in Vietnam, 123; and War of 1812, 19

Frankfurter, Felix, 79, 80

Franklin, Benjamin, 7, 15

free trade, 54-55, 59, 78

French Revolution, 15, 16, 24

Germany, 54, 55, 67, 117, 118, 147; Hitler as ruler of, 100, 101; reunification of, 143-144; during World War II, 77, 82, 85, 119, 144

Gettysburg, Battle of, 36, 38

Ghent, treaty signed at, 20

Gorbachev, Mikhail, 135, 141, 142, 143, 145

Grant, Ulysses S., 39, 48

Great Britain, 24, 29, 39, 40, 54, 55, 56, 60, 74, 84, 90, 103, 114; and arbitration of disagreements with U.S., 40-41, 43; Canada as possession of, 9, 19, 21, 22, 35, 41, 43; decline in power of, 77, 87; Hay as ambassador to, 49-53; navy of, 9, 18, 43, 70, 71, 73, 75; as nuclear power, 117; relations of, with U.S. during Civil War, 34-35, 36, 38; U.S. independence from, 7, 14; and War of 1812, 13, 15, 16, 17, 19-20; during World War I, 66, 100

Great Depression, 81

Greece, 9, 87, 88, 93

Greeley, Horace, 48

Greenland, 43

Gromyko, Andrei, 129

Gulf War, 149, 151

Haiti, 34, 43

Harding, Warren G., 68

Hatteras, 38

Hawaii, 42, 49, 53, 56

Hay, Augustus (brother), 46

Hay, Charles (father), 45

Hay, Clara Stone (wife), 49

Hay, Clarence Leonard (son), 55

Hay, Helen (mother), 45

Hay, John Milton: admiration of, for Lincoln, 46-47; as ambassador to Great Britain, 49-53; death of, 61; as diplomat, 47-48, 49; early years of, 45-46; Open Door Notes written by, 45, 55, 58-60; relationship of, with Seward, 45, 47, 49, 53; as secretary of state, 10, 45, 53-55, 58-60, 111

Hay, Milton (uncle), 45-46

Hay-Pauncefote Treaty, 60-61

Hitler, Adolf, 100, 101, 117-118, 144

Ho Chi Minh, 123

Holmes, Oliver Wendell, 80

Holy Alliance, 24, 26, 94

House of Representatives, U.S., 27, 30, 87

Hughes, Antoinette Carter (wife), 64, 73

Hughes, Charles Evans: attitude of, toward League of Nations, 68, 69; as justice of Supreme Court, 66, 75; death of, 75; early years of, 63-64; as governor of New York, 65-66; and negotiation of Five-Power Treaty, 70-71, 73, 74, 75; as presidential candidate, 66;

ABOUT THE AUTHOR

Jason Richie is the author of several titles from The Oliver Press, including *Secretaries of War, Navy, and Defense: Ensuring National Security*, *Spectacular Space Travelers*, *Space Flight: Crossing the Last Frontier*, and *Weapons: Designing the Tools of War*. A former noncomissioned officer in the U.S. Army, Richie graduated *summa cum laude* from the University of Minnesota with a degree in American history, which included a concentration of study on American foreign policy and European diplomacy. He lives in Houston, Texas, with his wife, Diana, and son, James.

PHOTO CREDITS

Archive Photos/Hulton Archive: pp. 26, 69, 85, 112, 123, 129, 131, 136, 143 (Reuters/Arthur Tsang), 144

Department of Defense: pp. 128, 149

Franklin D. Roosevelt Library: p. 104

George Bush Presidential Library: pp. 140, 141, 142, 145, 146, 148, back cover (top)

Harry S. Truman Library (National Park Service Photographs, Abbie Rowe): front cover (bottom left), pp. 91, 93

Library of Congress: pp. 2, 6, 8 (both), 14, 15, 16, 17, 18, 19, 20, 21, 23, 25, 27, 28, 31, 32, 33, 36, 37 (all), 39, 40, 41, 42, 44, 48, 52, 55, 56, 57, 58, 59, 60, 61, 62, 65, 67, 68, 71, 72, 73, 75, 76, 79, 81, 83, 84, 86, 90, 92, 96, 98, 101, 102, 106, 107, 108, 109, 110, 111, 115, 119, 120, 139, back cover (bottom)

MacArthur Memorial: p. 95

Minnesota Historical Society: pp. 12, 22, 50, 66, 126

National Archives: front cover (top right), pp. 11, 47, 51, 88, 116, 118, 122, 125, 132, 133, 134

PhotoDisc, Inc.: front cover (bottom right, both)

Revilo: pp. 35, 70

TASS: p. 114

United Nations: p. 99 (DPI Photo by Jullien)

University of Louisville Archives: p. 80

U.S. Naval Historical Center: pp. 38, 53

U.S. State Department: front cover (top left), pp. 150, 153, 154

The White House: p. 152